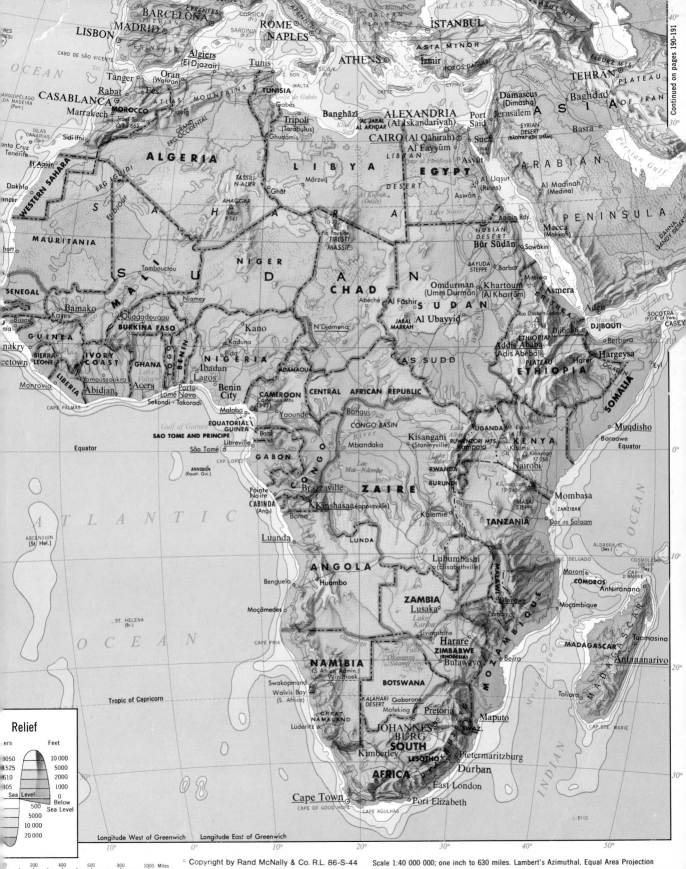

BLACK SEA

LISBON MADRID BARCELONA PYRENEES CORSICA (Fr.) APENNINES BALKAN PENINSULA İSTANBUL CAUCASUS MTS.

ROME NAPLES SARDINIA (It.) ADRIATIC SEA İzmir ASIA MINOR TOROS DAĞLARI ELBURZ MTS. TEHRÂN PLATEAU

ATLANTIC OCEAN CABO DE SÃO VICENTE Algiers (El Djazaïr) Tunis ATHENS CRETE Damascus (Dimashq) Baghdad OF IRAN

ARQUIPÉLAGO DA MADEIRA (Port.) CASABLANCA Tanger Oran (Wahran) Fès MALTA CYPRUS Jerusalem SYRIAN DESERT (BÂDIYAT ASH SHÂM) Basra

Rabat MOROCCO Golfe de Gabès Tripoli (Tarābulus) Banghāzi ALEXANDRIA (Al Iskandariyah) Port Said Suez ARABIAN Persian Gulf

ISLAS CANARIAS (Sp.) Marrakech Figuig Ghudāmis CAIRO (Al Qāhirah) Al Fayyūm Al Madînah (Medina)

Sidi Ifni ATLAS MOUNTAINS Jbel Toubkal 13,665 GRAND ERG OCCIDENTAL LIBYA EGYPT Asyūt Mecca (Makkah) DAHNA (SANDY DESERT)

Dakhla WESTERN SAHARA El Aaiún ALGERIA Mārzuq DESERT Al Uqsur (Ruins) PENINSULA

MAURITANIA ERG IGUIDI TASSILI-N-AJJER Ghāt Aswān Lake Nasser NUBIAN DESERT Admin. Bdy. Bûr Sūdan Sawākin

AHAGGAR Tahat 9,541 Pic Toussidé TIBESTI MASSIF 10,712 BAYUDA STEPPE Barbar Mitsiwa

SENEGAL Tambouctou NIGER CHAD Omdurman (Umm Durmān) Khartoum (Al Khartūm) Asmera ERITREA

Bamako Niamey Abéché Al Fāshir SUDAN Ras Dashen Terara 15,158

GUINEA Kano N'Djamena JABAL MARRAH Al Ubayyiḍ AS SUDD Djibouti DJIBOUTI Aden

BISSAU Kaduna Bida NIGERIA ADAMAOUA ETHIOPIAN PLATEAU Harer Hargeysa

SIERRA LEONE IVORY COAST GHANA BENIN Ibadan CAMEROON CENTRAL AFRICAN REPUBLIC ETHIOPIA OGADEN

Monrovia LIBERIA Lagos Benin City Cameroon Mtn. 13,451 Uele SOMALIA Eyl

CAPE PALMAS Acera Lomé Porto Novo Yaoundé Bangui Kisangani (Stanleyville) UGANDA Mt. Elgon 14,178 KENYA

Gulf of Guinea EQUATORIAL GUINEA Malabo Batá CONGO BASIN Mbandaka RUWENZORI MTS. Kampala Muqdisho

SAO TOME AND PRINCIPE Libreville CONGO River RWANDA Kisumu Nairobi Baraawe Equator

São Tomé GABON Lac Mai-Ndombe BURUNDI Kilimanjaro 19,340 Mombasa

ANNOBÓN (Equat. Gui.) CAP LOPEZ Brazzaville ZAIRE Kinshasa (Léopoldville) Ujiji MASAI STEPPE ZANZIBAR Dar es Salaam

Pointe Noire CABINDA (Ang.) Boma Kalemie TANZANIA ALDABRA IS. (Sey.) CAP D'AMBRE

ATLANTIC OCEAN ASCENSION (St. Hel.) Luanda LUNDA Lubumbashi (Elisabethville) MALAWI Moroni COMOROS Antsiranana

ANGOLA Huambo ZAMBIA Lilongwe Moçambique COSMOLEDO GROUP (Sey.)

ST. HELENA (Br.) Benguela Lusaka Lake Kariba Zomba MADAGASCAR Toamasina

Moçâmedes CAPE FRIA Livingstone Victoria Falls MOZAMBIQUE Beira Antananarivo

Tropic of Capricorn NAMIBIA (S. African Admin.) Okavango Swamp Harare ZIMBABWE (RHODESIA) Bulawayo

Swakopmund Windhoek BOTSWANA Gaborone Pretoria Maputo SWAZ.

Walvis Bay (S. African) KALAHARI DESERT Mafeking JOHANNESBURG LESOTHO Pietermaritzburg

Lüderitz GREAT NAMALAND Kimberley SOUTH AFRICA Durban INDIAN OCEAN

Cape Town CAPE OF GOOD HOPE CAPE AGULHAS East London Port Elizabeth

Equator Longitude West of Greenwich Longitude East of Greenwich

Relief

Meters	Feet
3050	10 000
4525	5000
610	2000
305	1000
Sea Level	0
500	Below Sea Level
5000	
10 000	
20 000	

Scale 1:40 000 000; one inch to 630 miles. Lambert's Azimuthal, Equal Area Projection
Elevations and depressions are given in feet.

Miles: 200 400 600 800 1000
Kilometers: 400 800 1200 1600

Enchantment of the World

SOUTH AFRICA

By R. Conrad Stein

Consultant for South Africa: John Rowe, Ph.D., African Studies Faculty, Northwestern University, Evanston, Illinois

Consultant for Reading: Robert L. Hillerich, Ph.D., Bowling Green State University, Bowling Green, Ohio

CHILDRENS PRESS ®

CHICAGO

Ostriches are raised on farms for their feathers.

Library of Congress Cataloging-in-Publication Data

Stein, R. Conrad.
  South Africa.

  (Enchantment of the world)
  Includes index.
  Summary: A look at South Africa, particularly the
present racial situation and its implications.
  1. South Africa—Juvenile literature.
[1. South Africa] I. Title. II. Series.
DT753.S73 1986   968   86-9651
ISBN 0-516-02784-0

Picture Acknowledgments
Nawrocki Stock Photos: 60, 62 (left); © **Jason Lauré:** 4, 10 (top), 16 (top & bottom right), 21 (left), 22 (left), 23, 27 (left), 30, 31 (2 photos), 33 (left), 37 (right), 38, 42, 43, 73, 75 (bottom), 76 (right), 85, 90, 91 (right), 94 (top right), 97 (right), 98, 106 (bottom right), 109 (left); **D.J. Variakojis:** 17 (right)
Chandler Forman: 122
Root Resources: © **Byron Crader:** 5, 10 (bottom), 26 (right); © **Dr. Martin M. Bruce:** 16 (left); © **Irene Hubbell:** 19 (bottom); © **John Hoellen:** cover, 70 (right), 95

Photri: 102 (left); © **J. Allen Cash:** 6 (2 photos), 8, 9, 14 (left), 17 (left), 20, 21 (right), 26 (left), 37 (left), 41 (2 photos), 51, 58, 76 (left), 86, 88, 89, 92 (bottom left), 97 (left), 99 (2 photos), 106 (top), 111
Stock Imagery: © **Charles G. Summers, Jr.:** 12, 93, 94 (bottom); © **Rita Summers:** 33 (right)
Valan Photos: © **Joyce Photographics:** 14 (right); © **Klaus Werner:** 72 (left), 92 (left center & right), 104; © **Peter Holland:** 96 (left)
R/C Agency: © **Richard L. Capps:** 19 (top), 27 (right), 94 (top left)
Tom Stack & Associates: © **Ann & Myron Sutton:** 22 (right); © **F.S. Mitchell:** 44 (bottom); © **C. Benjamin:** 72 (top right), 102 (right); © **Earl Kubis:** 91 (left)
Odyssey Productions: © **Robert Frerck:** 34 (2 photos), 44 (top), 70 (left), 72 (bottom right), 75 (top), 92 (top), 96 (right)
© **M. B. Rosalsky:** 47
Historical Pictures Service, Chicago: 52, 55, 61, 62 (right), 64, 65, 67
AP/Wide World Photos: 81, 83 (left & center), 84, 103, 109 (right)
Reuters/Bettmann Newsphotos: 82 (2 photos), 83 (right)
UPI/Bettmann Archives: 68 (2 photos), 83 (right), 106 (bottom left)
Len W. Meents: Maps on pages 12, 78, 92
Courtesy Flag Research Center, Winchester, Massachusetts 01890: Flag on back cover
Cover: Cape of Good Hope

A Zulu wearing a colorful costume

TABLE OF CONTENTS

Chapter 1

A COUNTRY OF CONTROVERSIES

At five in the evening in Johannesburg, South Africa, a visitor can stand atop one of the towering office buildings overlooking the train station and behold two streams of people flowing along the streets. On one street thousands of black men and women rush toward all-black trains that will carry them to all-black communities. Down another street white people hurry to all-white trains that run to all-white suburbs. Signs on the station walls mark the two entrances. One says COLORED or BANTU. The other says WHITES ONLY.

The scene at the railroad station is reminiscent of the era when European colonists were absolute masters over Africa, but preferred to keep at arm's length from the African people. The period of white colonialism in most of Africa ended a generation ago. Only in South Africa do whites legally continue to reign over blacks. And only in South Africa are the races kept apart by law.

South Africa is ruled by a racial minority. Whites are outnumbered almost five to one, yet they wield almost all the political power. Whites rule the economy, too. Although a few of the nation's blacks have grown rich, the vast majority live in

Opposite page: Johannesburg, built where gold was discovered, is the largest city in South Africa. After work, blacks catch transportation to return to their all-black communities.

A liquor store with separate entrances

poverty. Most whites, on the other hand, live an affluent life because South Africa is a fabulously wealthy country.

To protect their power and their privileged way of life, white South Africans have drawn up a complicated system of laws called apartheid. In the whites' Dutch-derived language the word means "apartness." Under the apartheid system blacks and whites cannot eat together in most restaurants, worship together in most churches, study in the same classrooms, or ride on the same buses. The rules of apartheid are slowly being revised, but political power remains in the hands of whites.

Blacks cannot vote in major elections. They have no legal way to change the system that treats them as aliens in the country of their birth. With no peaceful means to alter government policies, some blacks have turned to violence. Antigovernment demonstrations and riots in the past few years have claimed close to two thousand lives and captured world headlines.

South Africa's racial policies have made it one of the most

South Africa is a land of striking natural beauty.

universally despised nations on earth. The country is not a member of the United Nations, nor can its athletes compete in the Olympic games. Some foreign countries have limited trade with the nation. The quickest way to start an argument outside of South Africa among a group of college students—especially if that group includes a few black Africans—is to bring up the subject of apartheid.

But the furor surrounding apartheid has always masked another side of South Africa. It is far more than just a country of controversies. It is also a land of dazzling natural beauty, bountiful wealth, and surprisingly friendly people. A study of South Africa cannot ignore the racial laws that are condemned by practically all of the world's communities, but it would be a mistake to dwell on those laws alone. As the South African writer Alan Paton once said, "[South Africa] evokes something deep and powerful that satisfies even when it is painful, something exciting and depressing, attracting and repelling."

Above: Some national parks are designed to protect wildlife.
Below: Cape Town is situated on the Atlantic Ocean.

Chapter 2

A NATURAL
TREASURE TROVE

Probably no other nation on earth is more blessed by nature than South Africa. Its beauty is awesome. In some areas it is the Africa of fantasy, with rain forests and broad grasslands where wild animals roam freely. In other places it is mountains and seacoast meeting with breathtaking beauty. Only 15 percent of its soil can support crops, but South Africa grows more food than any other nation on the African continent.

Yet the heart of South Africa's riches lies below the ground, not above it. More than half the world's gold is mined in South Africa. To appreciate how rich in gold the country is, one can compare it to Canada, the world's fourth-largest gold producer. South Africa has one mine, near Johannesburg, that turns out more gold per year than all of Canada's mines together. In addition to gold, South Africa is the world's largest producer of diamonds. Some 85 percent of the world's supply of platinum comes from South African mines. Also the country is rich in uranium, copper, manganese, chromium, and coal.

The products of the mines, the farms, and an advanced factory system have given white South Africans a life of abundance undreamed of in most parts of poverty-stricken Africa. A gigantic gap exists between rich and poor and black and white, but the

Power plant

nation's overall prosperity is remarkable. Half the telephones in use on the African continent are found in South Africa. The country generates half the continent's electricity, manufactures 90 percent of its steel, and grows one fifth of its crops. All this from a nation that occupies only about 4 percent of Africa's land area and has about 6 percent of its people.

PROVINCES AND HOMELANDS

South Africa is situated at the extreme southern tip of the African continent. It spreads across 471,445 square miles (1,221,037 square kilometers), making it almost as large as the state of Alaska. At their greatest distances its borders run 1,010 miles (1,625 kilometers) from east to west, and 875 miles (1,408 kilometers) from north to south. The country has 1,650 miles (2,655 kilometers) of coastline.

The nation is divided into four provinces or states. They are the Cape of Good Hope Province (or Cape Province), the Transvaal, the Orange Free State, and Natal. These four provinces developed separately, but came together politically when the Union of South Africa was formed in 1910.

12

South Africa is one of the few countries in the world that claims more than one capital city. Officially it has three capitals. Its administrative capital is at Pretoria in the Transvaal. The legislative capital is at Cape Town in Cape Province. Finally, the country's judicial capital is at Bloemfontein in the Orange Free State. Most of South Africa's diplomatic offices are in Pretoria, and other nations generally regard that city as South Africa's capital.

As the southernmost country on the African continent, South Africa has the Atlantic Ocean on the west and the Indian Ocean to the south and southeast. Its northern neighbors are Zimbabwe, Botswana, and Namibia. In the northeast are Mozambique and Swaziland.

The independent state of Lesotho lies wholly within South African territory. Lesotho, which is about the size of the state of Maryland, is a mostly black kingdom that sits like an island in the southern part of South Africa.

The South African government claims four other independent states lie within its territory, but they are part of a controversial program called the homelands. The homelands are territories designated for black people. They came into being with the advent of apartheid laws.

LANDFORMS

There are no typical or uniform landforms in South Africa. The countryside varies from deserts to forests to grasslands to icy mountain peaks.

Altitude more than any other factor determines the landscape. The key word in defining the nation's landforms is "veld." In the Dutch-derived language it means grasslands, or land. The "high

A pine forest in the Transvaal (left) and Albert Falls in Natal

veld'' is found in a huge plateau that dominates the center of the
country. The plateau's average altitude is from 4,000 to 6,000 feet
(1,219 to 1,829 meters) above sea level. The ''middle veld''
surrounds the great plateau and supports many thriving farms.
The ''low veld'' lies at sea level and includes the tall grasslands
and brush where the country's herds of wildlife roam.

Deserts spread over much of the western portion of the nation.
A trackless yet fascinating desert is found in Cape Province. The
ancient South Africans called this desert the Karoo, meaning
''land of thirst.'' The Karoo is mostly a rocky wasteland where
only desert brush grows, but after just the slightest rainfall it
explodes into a brilliant tangle of wild flowers.

The eastern half of the country contains a spellbinding variety
of landscapes. Along the Indian Ocean coastline stand tropical
rain forests where towering hardwood trees are interlaced by
giant spiderwebs of vines. Some fifty miles (eighty kilometers)
inland the jungle gives way to patches of stately pine trees

growing among rolling hills. Beyond the pine forests spread parched brown mountains, which rise like sand castles in the air.

CLIMATE

South Africa has a pleasantly warm climate. Only the high veld experiences long periods of below-freezing temperatures. The nation's largest city, Johannesburg, has a significant snowfall about once every five years. When snow does pile up there, an unusual scene occurs. Instead of making snowmen, the black children who live in the townships that cluster around Johannesburg fashion figures of deer out of the snow. No one can explain how, when, or why this practice began.

South Africa lies in the Southern Hemisphere. The South African winter starts in May and runs through September. Spring arrives at the same time North Americans and Europeans are experiencing fall chills.

Altitude determines extremes of temperature in most of the country. Some lofty mountains are snow covered the year around. Hot, tropical weather prevails near the ocean at sea level. At one mountain spot in Cape Province, a person can start the morning skiing on a snow-covered slope, then drive south and spend the afternoon swimming in the warm currents of the Indian Ocean.

The country is often troubled by lack of rainfall, and the drought that struck the lower half of Africa in the mid-1980s affected South Africa. Crops failed, adding to the miseries of the impoverished black farmers who work marginal land.

Scant rainfall in the interior has left South Africa with no large lakes and only two significant rivers. No river is deep enough to allow traffic of large boats.

South Africa has over twenty thousand indigenous species of flowers including the protea (above left).

TREES AND PLANTS—A PARADISE IN GREEN

In the 1780s a French explorer named Francois le Vaillant passed through the South African wilderness near the Indian Ocean coast and wrote, "The flowers grow there in millions, the mixture of pleasant scents which arises from them, their color, their variety, the pure and fresh air which one breathes there, all make one stop and think nature has made an enchanted abode of this beautiful place."

South Africa's national flower is the fascinating protea, which grows there in many varieties. The flower was named after the Greek god Proteus, who had the remarkable power to change appearance. In an instant Proteus could become a dog, a crocodile, a tree, a rock, or a soaring bird. Considering the infinite species of plants and trees that thrive in South Africa, it was wise of the people to choose the protea as the symbol of their country.

A stinkwood forest (left) and baobab trees (right)

Ancient hardwood forests stand along the Indian coast. Prominent in them is a tree the early settlers called the stinkwood. Despite its name the tree has no odor, but when the wood is sawed it gives out a strong, pungent smell. Today stinkwood trees are protected by law. The trees, which mature at the age of five hundred years, have lost their ability to reproduce because the insect that pollinates their seed has died out. Another hardwood tree, called ironwood, is among the densest and heaviest woods that nature produces. South African ironwood is one of the few natural woods too heavy to float in water.

A totally bizarre tree grows in the sprawling grasslands of the low veld. European pioneers in South Africa were stunned when they first saw the baobab tree. They thought the tree had somehow grown upside down, with its roots rather than its branches spread in the air. Baobabs still stand like silent lords over the grasslands. They have trunks so thick that in some cases their girth exceeds their height.

WILDLIFE

A visitor fresh off the airplane, walking the streets of
Johannesburg, is forced to dodge swirling traffic while staring up
at the tall glass and steel buildings. It is difficult to realize that just
a one-hour plane ride from this modern city lies a piece of
storybook Africa where roaring lions and lumbering elephants
still roam. This wonderland of wildlife is called Kruger National
Park.

The huge park stretches 200 miles (322 kilometers) by 40 miles
(64 kilometers) and in area is about the size of the state of
Massachusetts or the country of Israel. The parkland is made up of
high grasses dotted by groves of thorn trees. Geographers call this
type of land savanna, but South Africans usually refer to it as the
"bush veld." A tangle of rivers and streams twists through the
grasslands and flows into lazy lagoons and swamps. This
combination of grass and water makes Kruger a perfect sanctuary
for African wildlife.

The wild animals delight the more than 400,000 tourists who
visit the park each year. Most tourists who visit South Africa are
white Europeans and Americans. Black travelers generally keep
away from the country to avoid being humiliated by the apartheid
laws. Also South African authorities deny visas to foreign blacks
who they fear would be "troublemakers."

Visitors usually see the sights of Kruger while riding in buses.
They sometimes complain of stiff necks because the tour guide is
constantly calling out, "Look to your left. Two elephants. Now,
over to your right. Look there! A herd of water buffalo."

Of all the animals in Kruger, none thrills the tourist more than
the lion. There are only 1,500 of them in the park, so when they

Visitors can drive through Kruger National Park (above) and see
a great variety of animals, including antelopes (below) at a watering hole.

The lions look harmless, but visitors are cautioned about possible danger.

are spotted lazing in the sun it often causes a traffic jam. Lions in the wild are best observed from a bus or a land-roving car. Vehicles can get closer to a lion than a person on foot can because the gasoline smell masks the human scent. Also, anyone trying to approach a lion on foot is risking his or her life, as the beasts are unpredictable.

Officials at Kruger admit they manage the park's environment rather than let nature take its course. All the 7,520 square miles (19,477 square kilometers) of parkland are enclosed by an enormously long cyclone fence. "The fencing is absolutely necessary to protect the animals from poachers and other dangers," says John Verhoef, a conservation officer. "But the barrier means [the animals] can no longer migrate, which is what their instinct tells them to do when water or a food supply is exhausted. Since humans have made it impossible for nature to have a free rein, we have to try to stimulate the natural environment the best we can." The stimulation includes pumping water into lagoons during a time of drought. Wildlife management also means the painful duty of killing animals when

Elephants and zebras also live in Kruger National Park.

officials deem a certain species has increased in number beyond what the parkland can support. Men flying in helicopters shoot the excess animals with darts containing a fast-acting poison.

South Africa has nine other major national parks. Karoo National Park features the haunting landscape of the great Karoo Desert. Rare forms of wildlife such as the black-footed wildcat live there. Mountain Zebra National Park was established specifically to protect the Cape Mountain zebra, which until recently was an endangered species. In the Tsitskama Forest National Park stand stately hardwood trees.

Smaller parks and game reserves are scattered about the country. And many species of African wildlife still roam freely in the nation's rural areas. In the near suburbs of Cape Town wild baboons sometimes swarm atop slow-moving commuter buses. Signs saying DON'T FEED THE BABOONS are as common in South Africa as KEEP OFF THE GRASS signs are in the United States.

Left: Pouring rough gold
Right: The big hole in Kimberley yielded tons of diamonds.

THE MINES—A SUBTERRANEAN TREASURE CHEST

Diamonds were discovered in South Africa in 1867, and from all over the world a horde of fortune seekers flocked to the land. From the largest hole ever dug by humans a priceless three tons of diamonds was carefully extracted. The water-filled pit, a mile (1.6 kilometers) around and half again as deep, can still be seen near the city of Kimberley. Sometimes a white South African will point to it and announce to a foreign visitor, "My forefathers dug that." In truth the awesome hole was scooped out by black laborers digging under the watchful eyes of white miners.

An even richer diamond mine began later near Pretoria. Several diamonds found there were as big as a fist, but diamonds are only a small part of the treasure that lies beneath South Africa's soil.

In 1886 gold was found at a dusty hillside in central Transvaal. Once more eager prospectors hurried to South Africa. Practically

Mining gold

overnight the barren hillside became a bustling camp of 100,000 rowdy miners. The camp grew into Johannesburg—South Africa's largest city.

Gold is still extracted from mines near Johannesburg, and the metal dominates the life of the city. Downtown streets bear such names as Claims, Nugget, and Quartz. A shift in the international price of gold—even just a few pennies an ounce—makes headlines in the city's newspapers.

Coal, copper, and uranium are less exciting than diamonds and gold, but those minerals also contribute to the national treasure chest. Thousands of men and women work in South Africa's vast mining industries. Johannesburg is the headquarters for some incredibly powerful mining companies, including the Anglo American Corporation, one of the richest business enterprises on earth.

Chapter 3

THE PEOPLE AND
THEIR INSTITUTIONS

For centuries South Africa has been a meeting ground for many races. Very early in its history the country was inhabited by a smattering of brown-skinned people. Then black people migrated from the north. Hundreds of years later whites landed from the sea and established a base at the very tip of the nation. Asians followed the whites. The various groups met, fought, merged, and made South Africa the multiracial land it is today.

When apartheid laws were enacted beginning in 1948, the white-dominated government divided its tangle of peoples into four racial categories: the blacks (who are also called the Africans), the whites, the colored (who are a mixture of white and nonwhite bloodlines), and the Asians. The government thus created a racial pyramid. At the peak of the pyramid stand the whites, who control the country's wealth and political power. Next are the colored and Asian races, who are looked upon as second-class citizens. At the base of the pyramid are the blacks. They cannot vote, rarely earn more than subsistence wages, and are treated as aliens in the land of their birth.

The estimated 1986 population of South Africa stood at 33,185,000. Using the government-created categories, 71 percent of the people were black, 17 percent were white, colored made up 9 percent, and Asians 3 percent. In the view of South African authorities, each race must occupy its own place on the pyramid steps. However, the splintering of the South African people goes even deeper than the laws laid down by its leaders. In this divided land even the racial divisions are divided.

THE BLACKS

With more than 21 million people, blacks (or Africans) comprise the largest single race in South Africa. But they are not a unified body. The blacks come from dozens of ethnic groups and subgroups, which speak different languages and lead different ways of life. The major ethnic groups are the Zulus, the Xhosa, the Sotho, the Tswana, the Shangan, and the Swazi. The Zulus and the Xhosa are the most numerous of these peoples, and both groups have roots that reach deep into South Africa's past.

At one time the Zulu people were the most feared warrior nation in all of southern Africa. A military genius named Shaka led the Zulus to stunning victories in a series of wars fought in the early 1800s. Later warrior-kings fought against whites. Armed mainly with spears, Zulu fighting men defeated a British army equipped with the latest rifles.

Today the Zulus are a peaceful, farming people who live mainly in the state of Natal. They still carry the look of warriors, however, standing tall, trim, and muscular. Rival ethnic groups resent the Zulus because of the aristocratic air they maintain. Their looks, their manners, and their bearing seem to convey a silent boast, "We are a people born to lead."

Sadly the economics of the 1980s has weakened the Zulu

Zulus are the largest ethnic group of blacks. Left: A Zulu woman   Right: A Zulu dance team

group's structure. There are more than five million Zulus, and their land cannot support their numbers. Men of working age must live and hold jobs in the cities and send money home from their weekly paychecks. They visit their wives and children only three or four times a year. A crusty old man standing outside his beehive-shaped house lamented this absentee father situation when he told a visiting journalist, "[The city] is a bad place for young men. They lose their sense of obedience and drink whiskey and adopt the ways of the white man."

The people known as the Xhosa are close neighbors to the Zulus. Numbering 2.5 million, the Xhosa are the nation's second-largest culture group.

The Xhosa used to entertain a belief that all the world's cattle belonged to them. In their traditions cattle rustling was considered to be a heroic act. Songs were sung and dances performed to

Many Xhosas have left their traditional lands to work in the cities.

honor brave and clever cattle raiders. Naturally the Xhosa's practice of stealing cattle made them unpopular neighbors. Gory battles raged between the Xhosa and white settlers in the 1800s.

Long ago the Xhosa gave up their practice of cattle raiding and they now live in harmony with their neighbors. They are a rural people whose dwellings are usually round huts covered by thatch roofs. Wandering near the huts are ever-present herds of cattle. Children have the task of keeping the cattle clustered in a herd. Any animal with a sudden urge to roam will be chased back promptly by a nimble ten year old.

Even more than the Zulus, the Xhosa people have left their traditional territory to find work in the cities. It is estimated that more than half the Xhosa live away from their original homes. Xhosa men have a reputation as excellent miners. Thousands now work in South Africa's vast mining system.

Blacks leaving their designated territories to work in the cities have given rise to a whole new subgroup called the urban blacks. Urban blacks number in the millions. They live in townships outside of South Africa's great cities and work in the urban factories. The urban blacks are another headache for South Africa's white leaders, who are determined to sort out their country's complex groups of people and tell each group where it must or must not live.

The urban blacks and the various ethnic groups are united against apartheid. Beyond that, however, blacks are a divided people, and sometimes dangerously so.

Buried among reports of antigovernment demonstrations was this news item carried by the wire services in May, 1985: "WELKOM, South Africa—Feuding Xhosa and Basothu tribesmen clashed at a gold mine where they worked, leaving 19 dead and 36 injured, a mine spokesman said Sunday. 'The men fought with sticks and stones and anything else they could lay their hands on,' said James Duncan, a spokesman for the Anglo American Corp., which owns the President Bond Mine 120 miles [193 kilometers] south of Johannesburg. . . .Mine security officials broke up the battle by firing tear gas."

This clash is a bloody example of the intergroup rivalries that plague South Africa and most of the African continent. Friction between African culture groups is often called tribalism. The statesman Felix Houphouet-Boigny, first president of the Ivory Coast, once said, "Tribalism is the scourge of Africa."

Blacks and whites have opposite opinions over the dangers of tribalism in South Africa. The whites claim that if the blacks ever assumed power their feuds would bring chaos and violence to the nation. The blacks say that this opinion is not only wrong but is used by whites as still another excuse to deny black people a political voice. The blacks point to Kenya, an African country containing many rival ethnic groups, yet one that has enjoyed peace and stability during thirty years of black rule.

Finally, many blacks admit they are a divided people, but they point out that the whites are split into two rival factions, also. In fact, scores of black leaders insist that the differences between the black culture groups are no greater than those that exist between the two major white factions.

THE WHITES

Just outside the city of Pretoria rises the most imposing monument built anywhere in Africa in the twentieth century. Called the Voortrekker Monument, it commemorates the one-hundredth anniversary of the Great Trek of 1836 to 1838. During that celebrated time in South Africa's past, offspring of the country's original white settlers journeyed across a hostile wilderness to carve out a new land. The monument is surrounded by a ring of bronze covered wagons called a "laager." In the old days white pioneers fought blacks from within a laager, and the circle of wagons remains an important symbol of the country's past. A typically South African sign posted at the entrance to the monument (it was removed in the early 1980s) read:

Visiting Hours-Whites Daily, 0900-1645

Non-Whites Tuesday, 0830-1200

The Voortrekker Monument is the great patriotic shrine of those whites called Afrikaners. They are descendants of the original Dutch, German, and French people who established a settlement at the Cape of Good Hope in the 1600s.

Sculpture of a wagon used in the formation of a laager.

Afrikaners make up 60 percent of the white population. Traditionally they were farmers, but today they have branched into practically every area of the work force. Most important, Afrikaners dominate the political process of the country. They are the authors of apartheid and stand as the system's most loyal defenders. Critics say the Afrikaner has a "laager mentality," a mind closed to any fresh idea or suggestion of change. Afrikaners claim they are acting to preserve their three-hundred-year-old cultural traditions.

Unlike other whites living on the African continent, Afrikaners are not ex-colonists. They have no loyalties to another state nor do they have a home country to escape to in case South Africa plunges into a racial war. They claim their forefathers arrived at South Africa's southern shores even before the blacks pushed down from the north (although historians have disproved this contention). Afrikaners believe they are as African as are the Zulus, the Xhosa, or any other black group. Afrikaners are sometimes called the "White Tribe of Africa," and they have no objection to that title.

Above all, the Afrikaners are romantics. They glory in their past

Left: Afrikaners at a political rally   Right: English-speaking whites

and look upon the time of the Great Trek as an almost mystical Golden Age. As the writer Sheila Paterson said, the Trek was a time "when land was there for the taking, where the veld grass grew tall, where the fountains never failed and the game thundered in uncounted herds. A life where men were strong and God-fearing, their women fair and brave, and Kaffir [the black] knew his place."

The second major white group is called (for lack of a better name) the English-speaking whites. They originated in Great Britain and, by Afrikaner standards, are latecomers on the continent. Most of their ancestors arrived in the country during the diamond and gold rush days. The highly educated English-speakers grasped control of the South African economy, and it used to be said that the British ran commerce and industry while the Afrikaners directed the government. This is less true today because Afrikaners have moved into the realm of big business.

The Great Boer War, fought from 1899 to 1902, pitted the forces of Great Britain against the Afrikaners. For decades after that war, resentment seethed between the two groups of white people. Now, however, there is a greater sense of unity between Afrikaner and English-speaking whites than ever before in the country's history. The two groups see themselves as crew mates on a tiny boat that is floundering about on a sea of black unrest.

Other whites living in South Africa include Portuguese, Germans, Greeks, and Italians. Many of these people migrated to the country in the years after World War II. There is also a Jewish community that numbers more than 100,000 people.

THE COLORED

Of all the classifications in South Africa's complex system of racial separation, the colored (mixed-race people) are the most difficult individuals for an outsider to identify. The colored are a blending between white-, brown-, and black-skinned people. Their looks and skin colors run the spectrum from fair hair with light skin to dark skin with negroid features. On a crowded street filled with different racial types, only another South African can tell at a glance whether a person whose features are borderline is classified black, white, or colored. And even the native South African will often be wrong.

Since 1950 every South African resident has been placed in one of four racial categories. Most people's classifications were obvious, but borderline colored posed a problem. Judges sometimes used bizarre tests to make a final racial determination of a borderline case. One method was the "pencil in the hair" technique. The judge put a pencil vertically in a borderline person's hair, and if the pencil remained standing upright the hair was determined to be "crinky," and the person was classified as black. If the pencil fell, the person was judged to be colored.

There are 2.5 million colored people living in South Africa. Almost 90 percent of them reside in Cape Province. Traditionally,

These children are classified as colored.

mixed-race people had close ties to the Afrikaners, speaking their language and worshiping at a sister branch of their church. The Afrikaners treated mixed-race people like cousins who had the misfortune to be born into the poor side of the family. In the racial pecking order, colored people were given positions in the work force above the blacks, but far below the whites. In return for these "favors" the colored were generally reluctant to oppose the white Afrikaners.

Today, however, more and more mixed-race people have aligned themselves with the blacks, and have become staunch opponents of white leadership. One of the spokesmen of the colored race is a fiery minister and scholar named Allan Boesak. He urges resistance against white government and calls those colored who remain loyal to the system "the junior partners in apartheid."

Finally, the existence of the colored race is an embarrassment to the Afrikaner. For generations the races had mingled in South Africa, and the colored people are the result. The Afrikaner is the loudest advocate of "keeping the races pure," but ironically he has probably less "pure white" blood than his English-speaking countryman. The odds are overwhelming that any white family

Indians at the market (left) and in a shop (right) in Durban

that has lived in South Africa for more than two centuries must, mathematically, have some colored blood in its heritage.

THE ASIANS

Some 800,000 people classified as Asians live in South Africa. Most of them reside in the state of Natal. Durban, Natal's largest city, is more than half Asian. By far the majority of South Africa's Asians originated in India.

The first Indians arrived in South Africa in 1860 when white farmers in Natal imported them to serve as laborers in the sugarcane fields. Later arrivals were better educated and had sufficient funds to set up small shops. The Indian-owned shops thrived and soon competed with white stores. The white-run government countered by passing laws restricting the activities of Indian residents. Challenging these laws was the courageous Indian-born lawyer Mohandas K. Gandhi, who arrived in South Africa in 1893 and stayed for twenty-one years. Gandhi led a nonviolent campaign that eventually reformed some of the anti-Indian laws. He became a hero in the Indian community, where the people called him Mahatma (great soul).

Traditionally, white leaders relegated Asians to a second-class status, and the Asians resented the government. But in the post-World War II era, many Indians achieved middle-class status and a few grew rich. Today most older-generation Indians are reluctant supporters of apartheid because they fear black political power would upset their comfortable way of life.

LANGUAGES

A typical telephone conversation between two Afrikaner farmers might go like this: "Hello. *Hoe gaan dit?* (How are you?) That's good to hear. *Hoe gaan dit mit die gesin?* (How's the family?) Great, that's good news!"

In the course of everyday conversation, the Afrikaner swings back and forth between his own language (called Afrikaans) and English, hardly noticing the difference. Afrikaans is a colorful language that is derived from Dutch, but contains words from German, French, English, and several African languages. It is spoken only in South Africa, primarily among the Afrikaners and the colored people. English-speaking whites learn Afrikaans at school, but only a handful of them are comfortable with the language.

South Africa uses Afrikaans and English as its two official languages. Signs in railroad stations and public buildings are posted in both tongues. Billboards blare out ENJOY COCA-COLA and under it the words *GENIET COCA-COLA*. The dual language system extends to television. On Mondays the first half of evening television is conducted in Afrikaans while the second half is rendered in English. On Tuesdays this schedule is reversed so English is first, and so on.

Aside from Afrikaans and English, eight major black African languages are spoken in South Africa. They can be divided into two related groups, the Nguni and the Sotho. For example, the Zulu and the Xhosa people speak Nguni tongues. The Nguni languages are characterized by an odd but strangely melodic clicking sound. The clicking comes when a speaker pronounces *c*'s, *x*'s, or *q*'s. For example, if a man says, "I am an Xhosa," it comes out, "I am an CLICK-osa."

Urban blacks, especially those who travel often between rural territories and suburban townships, have become amazing linguists. Many speak the language of their culture group, the language of their neighbors' culture group, plus English, plus Afrikaans.

RELIGIONS

There is a large degree of religious freedom in South Africa, and dozens of different faiths are practiced. Originally, black South Africans followed traditional religions. Their beliefs varied, but they generally included the acceptance of a single creator and the existence of powerful spirits that can work either good or evil upon man. Spiritual forces, capable of bringing good or bad fortune into a person's life, can lurk on a treetop, under a rock, or in the body of a bird or a lion. The most powerful spiritual forces come from the souls of dead family members and village elders.

Followers of traditional religions often seek the advice of persons called diviners, who are believed to have mystical powers and can ward off evil spirits while channeling positive forces into their lives. The diviners claim to be masters of the supernatural. To the African traditionalist the supernatural world is just as real and as solid as the ground he walks upon.

Left: An Anglican church in Port Elizabeth   Right: A shop selling herbs used by spiritualists

By far the majority of black South Africans practice Christianity. With 11 million members, the Methodist church has the largest black following. Other black Christians include 700,000 Lutherans, 800,000 Anglicans, 360,000 Presbyterians, and 1.6 million Roman Catholics.

Some of the country's Asians are Christians, but many practice the religions of the country of their origins. The Asians are either Hindu (70 percent), Muslim (20 percent), or Buddhist or Christian (10 percent).

White religious preferences are split primarily along ethnic lines. Most Afrikaners are members of the Dutch Reformed Church. English-speaking whites tend to join the Anglican or Methodist churches. Other whites go to Roman Catholic, Lutheran, and Jewish services.

The Dutch Reformed religion was brought to the country by the first white settlers in the 1600s. Its tenets center around the beliefs of the theologian John Calvin, who inspired European religious thought in the sixteenth century. Calvin accepted the doctrine of

Bishop Desmond Tutu

predestination, the notion that certain people, even before their birth, were predestined to go to heaven while others were doomed to suffer hell fires. Eventually the Dutch Reformed Church of South Africa interpreted Calvin's ideas to mean that white church members were predestined to rule over all other races in their nation. Armed with these beliefs the South African Dutch Reformed Church has accepted the system of apartheid, while most Christian institutions (including Dutch Reformed Churches in other nations) have condemned it.

The Anglican church, which is the choice of many English-speakers, is far more accommodating toward blacks than is the Dutch Reformed Church. Anglican services are integrated, although most churches are attended predominantly by one racial group. Recently the Reverend Desmond Tutu became the first black Anglican bishop of Johannesburg. In 1984 Bishop Tutu won the Nobel Peace Prize for his efforts to bring nonviolent change to South Africa.

GOVERNMENT

South Africa has a parliamentary form of government, but one that gives its president great powers. The president heads the cabinet, which sets national policies. He is also the leader of the majority political party. Before 1984 the country's chief executive was called the prime minister. Also before 1984 Parliament was a single-house body and an exclusively white establishment. Only white people were permitted to vote in parliamentary elections.

In August 1984, South Africa held a highly emotional election to endorse a new constitution that would give a limited parliamentary voice to colored and Asian people. The new constitution created two separate chambers for colored and Asians, but insured that Parliament as a whole would still be dominated by white lawmakers. The voting was held amid predictions of national disaster. Conservatives (mostly Afrikaners) claimed the new constitution would mean the death of white culture. Voters approved the new constitution, and it went into effect in September 1984.

During the turmoil of the election the government made no hint about giving the vote to blacks. By government reasoning black people are not citizens of South Africa. They are all assigned citizenship in one of ten special "homelands," which are territories carved out at the time apartheid laws were passed.

In conducting its foreign affairs, the South African government considers itself to be a bulwark against a wave of communism sweeping over Africa. Citing its fight against communism the government clings to the impoverished but mineral-rich nation of Namibia, which lies on its northwestern border.

Namibia (once called Southwest Africa) was a German colony

before World War I. The old League of Nations made South Africa trustee over the territory in 1920. South Africa was instructed to promote the "best interests" of the Africans involved. Since World War II, the United Nations and the World Court have repeatedly ordered South Africa to withdraw its armed forces from Namibia. Also, a guerrilla war between the forces of SWAPO (Southwest Africa People's Organization) and the South African army has raged on and off for the past twenty years. Still Pretoria refuses to withdraw from the potentially rich state because South African leaders claim Communists would take over in their absence.

To carry out its foreign policy, South Africa relies on a highly disciplined and well-equipped army. All white males must serve a two-year term in the armed forces. Nonwhite volunteers also serve, but whites dominate the officer corps. Since most countries refuse to sell weapons to South Africa, the nation has designed and built its own tanks and armored personnel carriers. Military experts claim the South African regular army is one of the finest in the world.

THE ECONOMY

South Africa's underground wealth remains the heart of its economy. Gold amounted to half the dollar value of its exports in 1984. The nation also mines diamonds, asbestos, coal, chromite, copper, manganese, platinum, silver, and uranium. South Africa's soil contains practically every mineral resource useful to man except oil.

The country is less fortunate in the richness of its farmland. More than 80 percent of the land is unsuitable for large-scale commercial farming. A chronic lack of rainfall plagues farmers.

Left: Irrigating farmlands   Right: Shearing merino sheep

But wealthy farm owners employ modern irrigation techniques and produce bountiful harvests. South African farms grow more food than any other African country. The leading crops are corn, wheat, sugarcane, and fruit. Some sheep ranches spread over 10,000 acres (4,047 hectares). Wool is one of the nation's leading exports. Most of the large farms and ranches are owned by whites. Where black-owned farms exist, they average about fifty acres (twenty hectares) in size. Black farmers often work marginal land and grow only enough to meet their family's needs with little left over to sell.

With 1,650 miles (2,655 kilometers) of coastline, South Africa has a well-developed fishing industry. For many years it has ranked among the ten most important fishing nations in the world. The fishing grounds off South Africa are so rich that fishing fleets of foreign nations are attracted there, and there is a constant danger of overfishing.

A worker in a hydraulic plant

South Africa has the most advanced factory system on the African continent. Principal products are clothing, processed food, chemicals, iron and steel, and machinery. Many factories are owned by giant European and American corporations. Blacks make up the bulk of unskilled and semiskilled factory workers, and over the years the effect of apartheid has been to keep their wages low. Meagerly paid workers and low taxes have meant hefty profits for foreign investors.

In the field of transportation, South Africa boasts 200,000 miles (321,867 kilometers) of roads and 14,000 miles (22,531 kilometers) of railroad track. The train system is government owned, and passengers are strictly segregated. Generally entire trains are reserved for whites or nonwhites only. Even the platforms where passengers wait for trains are separated and marked with signs reading WHITES ONLY or COLORED. Often the word *colored* in signs refers to all nonwhites.

During the 1960s and 1970s the South African economy experienced rapid growth. Few black people had a share in the wealth, but white workers and the white middle class enjoyed a

The Blue Train travels between Cape Town and Pretoria.
It is shown above going through the Karoo Desert.

standard of living unrivaled anywhere in the world. The 1980s, however, saw unemployment, a crippling inflation, a growing national debt, and the collapse of the country's currency (the rand). In 1985 the rand dropped to a low point of 35 cents to the United States dollar. Just two years earlier one rand was worth slightly more than one dollar.

The declining international price of gold was a major reason for South Africa's economic troubles, but dwindling foreign investment was a factor, too. In the United States and Europe many corporations were pressured by antiapartheid citizens' groups to divest their holdings in South Africa. Also, investors became reluctant to put money into South Africa's economy because they feared a racial war would paralyze the country.

Finally, in the 1980s big business and the government had to cope with increasing demands from black labor unions. Blacks were forbidden to form trade unions until the late 1970s, but union power has mushroomed in a short time. Black workers will no longer accept low wages while corporations reap great profits. The union of black miners is particularly strong. Black labor unions have also become a political force against apartheid laws.

The Khoi Khoi and San were some of the early settlers in South Africa. Some San rock art (above) has been found near Johannesburg. Below: Cleaning animal skins.

Chapter 4

SETTLING THE
DISTANT LAND

Even in the jet age a flight from New York to Johannesburg takes sixteen restless hours. Three centuries ago a sea voyage from a European port to Cape Town lasted six months or longer. Perhaps because of the country's vast distance from Europe and America, South African whites often operate as if they are stuck in a previous era. Yet South African history is unique among nations. At times it seems that the nation's past did not merely unwind but was carefully plotted and penned by a master storyteller.

EARLY SOUTH AFRICA

Thousands of years ago the southern tip of Africa was settled by two groups of brown-skinned people called the San and the Khoi Khoi. The San lived by hunting and gathering, while the Khoi Khoi raised sheep and cattle. When the whites arrived they called the San the Bushmen and the Khoi Khoi the Hottentots. The names Bushmen and Hottentots are now derogatory terms.

The life-style of the San required that they live in close harmony with nature. They were experts on plant and animal life, and they practiced conservation of their scarce resources. The San left intricate rock paintings, which can still be seen on cave walls. It is supposed the San and the Khoi Khoi, original settlers of South Africa, lived a relatively peaceful life in a sunny land that teemed with game, wild fruits and berries, and fish. But their pastoral way of life was disturbed by invasions of tall strangers who closed in from both the north and the south.

A great migration of what historians call the Bantu-speaking people began in central Africa at the time of Christ. The Bantu-speakers (who are ancestors of today's black Africans) were farmers and cattle tenders who used iron to forge tools and weapons. Mile by mile and generation by generation they pushed east and south, absorbing or conquering the people who lay in their path. Long before white seafarers ventured toward the Cape of Good Hope, the Bantu-speaking people occupied all of South Africa except for the western Cape region.

Some eight hundred years after the Bantu migration reached South Africa, mysterious large ships began plying the waters close to its beaches. The San and the Khoi Khoi were stunned to discover the men in those ships had skin as white as the desert sands.

THE FAIREST CAPE

According to tradition, the first European ship to round Africa was commanded by the Portuguese seafarer Bartholomeu Diaz in 1488. Diaz's ship was dashed about in a treacherous gale, so he called the tip of Africa the Cape of Storms. King John II of Portugal hoped Diaz had found a sea route to the East, so he renamed it the Cape of Good Hope. A century later the

The Cape of Good Hope was originally named the Cape of Storms.

Englishman Sir Francis Drake noted the astonishing beauty he found at the windswept Cape of Good Hope. Drake's log in 1580 contains this appreciation: "This Cape is the most stately thing and the fairest Cape we saw in the whole circumference of the earth."

Certainly the most overwhelming feature of the cape that so impressed Drake was the mighty peak called Table Mountain. As seen from shipboard the mountain rises gracefully 3,500 feet (1,067 meters) into the sky, then flattens out with surprising suddenness to form a lofty tabletop. In Drake's time and now, puffs of clouds roll in from the sea and hover over its flat peak, looking much like a spotless white cloth covering a giant table.

Before the cape area became a European settlement, ship captains regularly gave a piece of silver to the first deckhand to spot the amazing flat peak that seemed to have been planed by some celestial carpenter. On clear days it could be seen more than 100 miles (161 kilometers) out to sea. Below the mountain was Table Bay, a natural harbor where ships could put in.

For decades the remote cape was unclaimed by European powers, but the area was not untouched. The beach at Table Bay served as a makeshift post office. Sailors' voyages lasted several years, and they had no way to send mail home. So, along Table Bay sailors selected special stones, polished them, and chiseled instructions on their faces. Seamen heading east carefully placed letters under these stones. Sailors making their return trips toward Europe picked up the letters and mailed them when they reached their home ports. Several of these postal stones can be seen in South African museums.

As trade with the East increased, however, some shrewd businessmen in The Netherlands discussed putting a bold new enterprise on this "fairest of Capes."

EUROPEANS ON AFRICAN SOIL

In April 1652, three Dutch vessels under the command of Jan van Riebeeck dropped anchor at Table Bay. Some eighty men and a scattering of women and children boarded small boats and rowed to the lonely beach. This event, according to present-day Afrikaner thinking, was the beginning of South African history.

Their purpose was not to form a new European colony. Instead van Riebeeck was instructed to build a "refreshment station," which would provide vegetables, fruit, and fresh meat to passing ships. The landing party was commissioned by the powerful Dutch East India Company that controlled the rich tea and spice trade. Captain van Riebeeck was instructed to live in peace with the Khoi Khoi people near the fort and trade goods for their cattle. The hardworking Dutch built a strong fort. Remains of that fort can be seen today, displayed in a vast underground shopping center beneath central Cape Town.

Three events soon altered the life of the settlement. First, slaves were imported to the station from Java and Madagascar. Second, a handful of adventurous Dutch decided to drift away from the stockade walls and establish their own farms. They became South Africa's first "Boers" (the Dutch word for farmers). Third, the Khoi Khoi went to war against the whites who were encroaching on land that traditionally belonged to them. The Khoi Khoi were easily defeated by the whites' superior weapons and organization. It was the first of many such wars to come.

The year 1702 was the fiftieth anniversary of white settlement at the southern tip of Africa. By then the white population totaled fifteen hundred people. Most were Dutch, but two hundred French and a lesser number of Germans had joined the group. More than one thousand dark-skinned slaves lived among the settlers. The slaves were either Malayan or were Khoi Khoi women and children whose men had been killed in battles with the whites. Only a handful of the slaves were black Africans.

Already a new race that was darker than white and lighter than black had appeared. The new race was a mixture of white, Khoi Khoi, and Malay bloodlines. It was the precursor of today's colored people. Afrikaner preachers later pounded on pulpits and insisted that the colored race was the result of lusty sailors who stormed off their ships and grabbed the first women they saw, but in truth the original Dutch settlers mated freely with nonwhite women. Richard van der Ross, a South African historian who is a colored, says that the colored race began "nine months after the arrival of Jan van Riebeeck and his followers."

In their isolated corner of the world, the whites relied on their religion for comfort and security. As an outpost of Europeans in Africa, the Dutch began to believe they were a chosen race, much as were the Hebrew children in the Bible. This belief intensified as they fanned out to occupy a greater area of southern Africa.

Aside from the influence of religion, the pioneer history of South Africa is characterized by the restlessness of the hardy farmers called the Boers. A Boer was never satisfied until he had seen the land over the next hill, and then the hill beyond that, and so on. The most adventurous ones became known as "trekboers" (farmers on the move).

The trekboers' steady migration brought them deeper into the lands of the Khoi Khoi and the San. Frontier wars raged almost constantly. The trekboers enslaved defeated Khoi Khoi and hunted down the San with an almost sinister glee. One Dutch official complained that the wars against the San were "teaching our people to shoot down a fellow-being with as little compunction as they would a hare or a wolf."

In clashes with the whites, the San and Khoi Khoi were the ultimate losers. Those who survived frontier battles succumbed to smallpox, a disease brought to southern Africa by the Europeans. Eventually the San were driven to the Kalahari Desert, where they still live. The Khoi Khoi were gradually absorbed into white society, and disappeared as a distinct culture in the late 1800s.

By 1778, when the European colony was more than a century old, the trekboers reached the Great Fish River some 400 miles

Vineyards near Stellenbosch

(644 kilometers) from their starting point at Cape Town. The white population had swelled to fifteen thousand, and villages with names like Stellenbosch, Swellendam, and Uitenhage had sprouted up. The settlers spoke their own brand of Dutch. People fresh from The Netherlands complained they had difficulty understanding the language because it had so many foreign words.

The most powerful actor in the drama of South African history had yet to take the stage. Beyond the Great Fish River lived the black Bantu-speaking people. Like the trekboers they were farmers and herders. When the whites and blacks collided, a thunderclap sounded and its vibrations still echo over the land.

SHAKA OF THE ZULUS

A man who would electrify southern Africa was born in a Zulu village in the year 1786. At the time the Zulus were a tiny farming chiefdom that lived in constant fear of their more powerful Bantu-speaking neighbors. The child's name was Shaka, and his birth caused a scandal because he was said to be illegitimate. Other boys

Zulu warriors preparing for battle

teased him incessantly about his improper father, and Shaka grew up fighting. Perhaps the constant fighting toughened him, for when he reached his teens Shaka was lean and muscular with the reflexes of a cat and the strength and courage of a lion.

At age thirty Shaka became chief of the Zulus. With cruel but effective measures he transformed the simple farming people into a splendidly disciplined warrior nation. Shaka revolutionized African warfare by teaching his men to charge into enemy ranks and stab with a new short-handled spear that he designed, rather than hurl their weapons as was the custom. His chess-player mentality directed swift strikes on an enemy's flanks before launching a devastating frontal assault. Shaka never fought against whites, but had he lived long enough to confront them South Africa perhaps would be a different nation today.

With Shaka in command, the Zulu war machine was invincible. In a series of lightning attacks he defeated neighboring kingdoms and incorporated the survivors into the Zulu nation. In four years Shaka conquered a territory larger than France and commanded an army that numbered 100,000 men. He ruled as an absolute dictator. His mere glance could condemn a person to death. Out of fear and loyalty his soldiers would have charged off a cliff if their commander ordered it.

But Shaka, like Alexander the Great, was unable to conquer his own emotions. In his troubled childhood his mother was his only friend. When she died Shaka was unable to cope with the loss. To mourn her death Zulu territory people were forbidden, under pain of death, to milk cows or harvest crops. Shaka's grief so overcame him that he lost his keen sense of self-preservation. In 1828 his two half brothers stole up to the place where he sat, crying over his mother, and stabbed him to death.

During his era Shaka was not fully understood, nor is he now. Although he conquered black people, he believed his real enemies were the whites who were pushing up from the south. The ultimate goals of his conquests were black unity and preparation for the final battle between the races. According to his biographer, Thomas Mofolo, Shaka's dying words to his half brothers were, "You think you will become chief when I am dead. But it will not be so, for the white man is coming and you will be his slaves."

THE GREAT TREK

While Shaka carved out the Zulu Empire, stunning political changes swept Cape Town. Despite the colony's remoteness, European wars spilled over into South Africa.

In 1795 ships of the British navy landed at Table Bay, and British forces seized Cape Town. The British acted because they feared their rivals, the French, were poised to take over the Dutch settlement. In 1803 the British returned the colony to the Dutch, but reoccupied it three years later, this time for good.

At first this international jockeying failed to disturb the far-flung Boers. Separated from The Netherlands by thousands of miles and several generations, most Boers felt little loyalty toward their homeland. Certainly the farmers along the Great Fish River worried more about fighting Xhosa cattle raiders than what country's flag flew over Cape Town.

Soon, however, Great Britain imposed new laws on the settlement, and those laws altered the way of life from Cape Town all the way to the frontier.

In 1815 a Khoi Khoi servant approached a British judge and complained that his Boer master had treated him cruelly. Before British rule, such a complaint could never have been lodged. But the British (much to the horror of the old settlers) gave limited legal rights to the Khoi Khoi and the colored. The judge ordered the master arrested. The arrest was carried out by a white officer accompanied by twelve Khoi Khoi soldiers.

The Boers lived for generations in the religious belief of white supremacy. To them Khoi Khoi assisting in the arrest of a white man was an unthinkable sin. A gunfight broke out at the farm. This was followed by a short-lived revolt by the Boers against British rule. British soldiers quickly crushed the revolt, and five of the rebels were hanged at a place called Slagter's Nek. The Dutch-descended people considered the hangings to be an atrocity, and from that time on loathed British rule.

The British followed Slagter's Nek with other acts that infuriated the Boers. In 1828 the British governor declared English to be the only official language of the colony. That same year a new charter gave Khoi Khoi and colored people equal footing with whites. In 1834 the British abolished slavery. Finally the British army began punishing the trekboers who raided Xhosa territory for pastureland and cattle.

For thousands of Boers, life under British rule was the same as paying homage to the devil. Instead of submitting to the British,

Boers trekking to the Transvaal

they abandoned their homes, packed up their wagons, and set out toward new lands to the north and east. "We quit this colony under the full measure that the English government has nothing more to require of us," said the Boer leader Piet Retief, "and will allow us to govern ourselves without interference in the future."

The storied era in South African history called the Great Trek began.

From 1836 to 1838 the Boers traveled over the wilderness in small bands of wagons that trailed cattle, children, and dogs. Ahead lay hunger, disease, and Bantu people who might or might not be hostile. The trekkers marched into even greater perils than those faced by American pioneers entering the western frontier at almost the same time. But the Boers had a deep trust in their religion and a profound sense that they were exercising God's will.

THE COVENANT

The most famous trekkers were the band commanded by Piet

Retief, who led his people into Natal—the very heart of Zulu territory. Upon reaching Zulu land, Retief approached the Zulu king, Dingaan, and asked permission for his people to settle there. Retief had no idea that Dingaan was one of the cunning half brothers who had murdered Shaka nine years earlier.

Dingaan offered to discuss the request and invited Retief, his seventy Boer officers, and thirty San soldiers to a banquet. While the party ate, Dingaan suddenly shouted, "Kill the wizards!" From out of the bushes raced hundreds of Zulu warriors. Retief and his followers were clubbed to death. Then Dingaan ordered his soldiers to attack Retief's wagon train. Some three hundred Boer men, women, and children were killed.

Seeking revenge, the Boers sent a heavily armed wagon train into Zulu territory. It was commanded by Andries Pretorius (for whom the city of Pretoria was later named). The band of oxen-drawn wagons climbed to high ground near a broad river. There the sixty-four wagons formed a laager—that tight circle of wagons, each touching the next to make fortress wheels. The Boer fighting men stuffed thornbushes underneath the wagons and into all openings.

In their laager the Boers waited. They prayed to God to grant them a Covenant, a special agreement similar to the one He had given to the Hebrew people of old when they ventured into the alien land of the Canaanites. The Boers vowed that if God granted them victory in the coming battle they, in turn, would honor the day of that victory for all their generations to come. The prayer sessions reached mystical heights. For that handful of men, God was in their laager with them, waiting.

When the sun rose on December 16, 1838, the Boers were greeted by an awesome sight. Rank after rank of Zulu warriors—

some ten thousand strong—were poised to attack. One Boer later wrote, "The whole Zulu kingdom sat there." Screaming battle cries, waves of the splendid Zulu warriors rushed the laager.

The Boers, all splendid shots with their muskets, stood unwavering behind their ring of wagons and fired into the sea of attackers. Zulus in the front ranks fell by the hundreds, and warriors to the rear simply ran over their bloody backs. Had the military genius Shaka directed the attack, he might have dreamed up some method of reaching the laager without slaughtering his troops, but Dingaan's generals lacked Shaka's imagination. They simply sent waves of warriors forward in a suicidal frontal assault. Both sides fought with legendary bravery, but spears alone were no match against musket fire. At the end of the day three thousand Zulus lay dead. The river gushed red with their blood. Inside the laager, the Boers suffered only three wounded.

Never before in military history was a victory more one-sided. To the Boers it forever would be called the "Battle of Blood River." It was accepted as a clear sign that God had answered their prayers and granted them a holy Covenant.

Today December 16 is honored as the Day of the Covenant. It is the most spirited holiday on the Afrikaner calendar—a day when the people glory in their nationality. Critics may claim that present-day Afrikaners have a laager mentality that pits them against the rest of the world, but what do the critics know? A sacred Covenant was made at Blood River in 1838. According to Afrikaner thinking, God gave them their sunny land with the same almighty authority He gave the Hebrews the land of Canaan. And on this sacred day the Afrikaner will tell anyone who cares to listen that he will break the Covenant only at the cost of his eternal soul.

Diamonds were discovered in the Orange Free State in 1867.

Chapter 5

A MAGNET

FOR THE WORLD

In the latter half of the nineteenth century, the remote and backward land of South Africa amazed the world when diamonds and gold in huge deposits were discovered there. The sudden influx of fortune seekers and the overwhelming outpouring of greed created by the discoveries altered the South African way of life forever.

In the twentieth century the mortal defeat of the Afrikaner was followed by their dynamic rebirth. The modern era saw the blacks totally stripped of even their most basic rights as citizens. The world now awaits the next twist in the South African story.

SUDDEN RICHES

On a lazy summer day in 1867, a farm boy named Erasmus spotted a sparkling pebble near his home in the newly independent Boer area called the Orange Free State. He took the pebble to his mother, who smiled and put it on the kitchen shelf. A local peddler caught sight of the unusual stone and asked to take it to town. He suspected it might be valuable, but no one dreamed the stone was a diamond, because it was commonly

An old photo of the Kimberley Diamond Mines. The wires carried buckets filled with clay to the top.

believed diamonds were found only in India and Brazil. However, the stone proved to be a diamond, and South Africa would never again be the same.

From all over the world a horde of eager treasure seekers descended on a barren slope in the Orange Free State that had been occupied primarily by Khoi Khoi and colored people. In just five years the spot became the town of Kimberley, and eventually was the second-largest city in southern Africa. In less than a decade miners extracted $100 million in gems from the soil.

Mining boomtowns such as Kimberley usually produce hordes of losers and only a handful of winners. Two Englishmen to emerge as winners from the diamond madness were the adventurer Barney Barnato and the empire-builder Cecil Rhodes.

Barney Barnato grew up in a London slum. To earn a living he worked as a clown and a juggler at circuses. When he came to South Africa he saw miners frantically digging for diamonds in

Cecil John Rhodes

yellowish clay on the ground's surface. Barnato read reports that
suggested diamonds might also be found in bluish clay a few feet
under the surface. He played a hunch and won. Digging in the
bluish clay, Barnato was soon earning $10,000 a week.

Cecil John Rhodes was born into a middle-class English family.
He came to South Africa at age seventeen, hoping the dry climate
would cure his tuberculosis. Combining inexhaustible energy
with a certain mad genius he became a millionaire in the diamond
business. After several stormy meetings Rhodes bought out
Barnato's enterprises and formed the giant DeBeers Mining
Company. One check that changed hands between Rhodes and
Barnato totaled $26 million—probably the largest bank check ever
written up to that time.

His fortune secured, Rhodes turned to the pursuit of a strange
dream. In Rhodes's mind the progress of world civilization
demanded that the British Empire rule all of Africa, from the Cape
of Good Hope north to Cairo. To secure his dream, Rhodes used
his fortune to become prime minister of Cape Colony in 1890.

Left: Paul Kruger   Right: A cartoon showing Cecil Rhodes conquering the African continent

Standing in his way to transform all of South Africa into a British colony were the independent and unmovable Boers.

THE BOER REPUBLICS

Since the era of the Great Trek, the Boers had populated three independent states in southern Africa: the Transvaal, the Orange Free State, and Natal. Britain annexed Natal in 1843, but recognized the independence of the other two republics.

Within the confines of those states the Boers established their own culture, free from British domination. They forced local African people into unpaid labor. They practiced their religion, spoke their language, and began calling each other Afrikaners. Then gold was discovered on the lands claimed by the Afrikaner people, and once more the English coveted Boer settlements.

Leading the Afrikaners of the Transvaal was their president, Paul Kruger. At age ten Kruger had crossed the wilderness with his family as part of the Great Trek. He had little formal schooling, but was a Bible scholar and possessed a profound folk wisdom. He once was asked to settle an estate dispute between two brothers quarreling over shares of a farm left them by their father. Kruger said simply, "Let one brother divide the land, and the other take first choice."

Kruger looked upon the Boer Republic of the Transvaal as God's outpost in a world gone mad with greed. Every day hundreds of gold seekers, most of them from Great Britain, poured into the mining sites at Johannesburg. The Boers called these interlopers *uitlanders* (foreigners), heathens doing Satan's work. By 1895 some eighty thousand *uitlanders* resided in the Transvaal, and were thought to outnumber the Boers two to one. Kruger refused to grant the newcomers political rights. He also refused to visit Johannesburg, which he called "a devil's town."

Prime Minister Cecil Rhodes desperately wanted the British Empire to take over the Transvaal, and plotted a way to deal with Kruger and his stubborn Boer followers. In 1895 Rhodes sent a small private army, which he paid from his own enormous bankroll, to the Transvaal to overthrow President Kruger. The mission (called the Jameson Raid) was a colossal failure. Kruger remained in power, and proved to be the most dogged adversary Rhodes ever faced.

Because of the Jameson Raid, the presence of so many English-speaking foreigners, and the ever increasing territorial demands of the British, a terrible war broke out in 1899 between Afrikaners and the force of Great Britain. The war lasted until 1902.

THE GREAT BOER WAR

"This war," wrote the Afrikaner Hettie Domisse, "this Boer War was the stupidest war the English ever carried on, because all they achieved was to consolidate the Afrikaner Nation, from the bottom of the Cape, right up to the Transvaal."

Boer artillery in action

The war drew into its horrors many thousands of Afrikaner women and children. Memories of the war lingered and served as a great wedge that split the nation's white population for decades to come.

After the opening battles, Boers began hit-and-run raids on British outposts. British commanders found the raids impossible to stop. The Boer horse soldiers knew every hidden trail and each secluded canyon the veld had to offer. They stormed out of the countryside, struck, and then simply melted back into the fields. To counter the Afrikaner guerrilla tactics, the British high command decided to deny the Boers the support of the farms that fed and sheltered them. Systematically British soldiers blew up farmhouses, burned fields, and killed cattle. The women and children on the farms were rounded up and forced to live in tents within barbed-wire enclosures. Some historians have called these history's first "concentration camps."

Boer prisoners rounded up in the church square in Pretoria

In the camps the war took its ugliest turn. Sanitation facilities were almost nonexistent, and diseases ravaged the inmates. Food supplies were only marginal to begin with, and many Afrikaners refused to eat because they suspected the British were poisoning their meals. By the end of the Boer War 26,000 Afrikaner women and children had died in the camps.

Dreadful stories about the South African prison camps drifted back to England. An Englishwoman named Emily Hobhouse visited a camp and observed "a death rate such as had never been known except in the times of the Great Plagues. The whole talk was of death—who died yesterday, who lay dying today, and who would be dead tomorrow." These reports, combined with heart-wrenching newspaper pictures of Afrikaner children who looked like tiny skeletons, outraged British liberals.

Less well known in England was the fate of blacks who worked for and remained loyal to the Afrikaners. They were also removed from the farms. The men were forced to serve on British labor gangs. Their families were put in separate barbed-wire camps where they were fed even less than the Afrikaner women and children. As a result of the war some thirteen thousand blacks died.

The war took many strange twists of fate. Paul Kruger, aged and broken, left his beloved country and died in exile. Cecil Rhodes, though still a young man, died of a heart attack just months before the British flag waved triumphantly over all of southern Africa. And two young men who participated in the Boer War would later mold the twentieth century. Working as a stretcher-bearer was the Indian national, Mohandas K. Gandhi. As a pacifist he refused to take up arms. He would later free India from the British yoke and be hailed as the prince of peace in the modern era. Serving as a young army lieutenant was the future British Prime Minister Winston Churchill. He later brought his country out of the darkest hours of World War II and led it to final victory. Did the stretcher-bearer and the lieutenant cross paths on some lonely hill and perhaps catch each other's eye? Probably not, but history will never know for sure.

The end of the Boer War came in 1902, and left the British the uncontested masters of southern Africa. Two decades earlier the British army had defeated the Zulus, the last black nation to resist English rule. That war, though gory, was fought with both sides displaying remarkable heroism. The Boer War was barbaric by comparison.

The British victory led to political union. In 1910 the old Cape Colony joined with the newer republics of Natal, the Transvaal,

Louis Botha served as prime minister from 1910 to 1919.

and the Orange Free State to form the Union of South Africa. This Act of Union would have been impossible under the Boers, whose leaders constantly feuded with the British and with each other. The modern state of South Africa was a reality at last.

THE RISE OF AFRIKANER NATIONALISM

The British were generous in victory. After the war they granted full political rights to Afrikaners, something the Boers had steadfastly denied English-speaking residents. The British did this knowing that the Afrikaners held a majority in the country as a whole, and would certainly elect their own candidates as leaders. To reward their generosity the people chose Louis Botha as prime minister. Botha urged Afrikaners to forget the past and unite with the English-speaking people.

The country's next prime minister was an unusually gifted, multitalented Afrikaner named Jan Christiaan Smuts. Smuts was a lawyer, an authority on poetry, and an intellectual known for his profound speeches and his philosophical writing. In his first term

J.B. Hertzog (above) and Jan Smuts (right)

as prime minister Smuts served from 1919 to 1924. Like Botha he pursued a policy of reconciliation between Afrikaners and English-speaking whites. Meanwhile the voices of African people who cried out for political rights were ignored. Because he tried to bring the English-speakers and Afrikaners together the international community hailed Jan Smuts as a great humanitarian, but many of his fellow Afrikaners condemned the prime minister as a turncoat who sold out his own people.

During the administrations of Botha and Smuts, the conservative Afrikaners quietly formed the National political party. It was made up largely of old-line Boers who still called British-descended people *uitlanders,* and believed that granting rights and privileges to blacks was a heresy. In 1924 the National party joined with the Labor party and gained control over the government. The National party founder, J.B. Hertzog, became prime minister.

Hertzog led the government for the next fifteen years. He backed the Afrikaner causes, especially the subjugation of blacks.

When a liberal politician suggested that blacks deserved at least comparable pay with whites in the mining and railroad industries, Hertzog responded, "The Europeans must keep to a certain standard of living which shall meet the demands of white civilization. Civilization and standard of living always go hand in hand. Thus a white cannot exist on a native wage scale, because this means he has to give up his own standard of living and take on the standard of living of the native."

Hertzog especially championed the Afrikaner language, Afrikaans. Just after the Boer War British authorities had tried to wipe out the Dutch-derived tongue. At British-run schools Afrikaner children who dared use their native tongue were forced to stand in a corner holding a sign reading "I am a donkey. I speak Dutch." With the National party in command, Afrikaans was proclaimed, by law, equal to English.

While the National party moved publicly to achieve Afrikaner goals, a secret organization called the Broederbond (band of brothers) worked behind the scenes. Formed by conservative Afrikaners after World War I, the Broederbond was a shadowy group of businessmen, educators, politicians, labor leaders, and clergymen dedicated to shifting economic might as well as political power to the Afrikaner. Broeders directed business contracts, government promotions, and labor agreements into the hands of fellow members of the organization. The close-knit society gained enormous power over the nation's institutions.

A highlight of the Hertzog administration came in 1931 when Great Britain granted independence to South Africa, and the country became a partner in the British Commonwealth of Nations. This elevated South Africa to the same status as Canada, Australia, and New Zealand.

The Voortrekker Monument with a closeup (left) of the statue in the center

The one-hundredth anniversary of the Day of the Covenant came in 1938. To honor that heroic time thousands of Afrikaners traveled to the site near Pretoria where the Voortrekker Monument was later built. Many made the journey in ox-drawn wagons as their ancestors had done a century earlier. On December 16, the throng gathered on the hillside where they laughed, cried, prayed, and shared pride in their past glories and their present power. Once more the destiny of this marvelous land belonged to the Afrikaners, and they would never release their grip. While bands played, the thousands of men and women joined in singing their stirring Afrikaner anthem: "We shall live, We shall die, We for thee, South Africa."

Chapter 6

THE ERA OF APARTHEID

A black man identified only as "Lucky" recently told a foreign journalist, "You who are not even South African are freer to move around this country than I am. This is why we are frustrated here. Everywhere we turn we face restrictions and more restrictions."

APARTHEID

For South Africa the year 1948 opened a new chapter in the history of race relations. During the years of World War II the country was ruled by the aging statesman Jan Christian Smuts, but the 1948 elections brought the National party to power. Many of its leaders had been jailed by Smuts for being pro-Hitler. Under Nationalist Prime Minister D.F. Malan the notorious series of apartheid laws were enacted. To be sure, forms of racial segregation had been practiced in South Africa since the first Dutch settlement at the foot of Table Mountain. The new apartheid system made laws out of what had been customs and added some new elements.

Over all of South Africa the color line was drawn. Signs were posted telling blacks where they could and could not go. Writing in 1966, the black South African journalist Ernest Cole said, "To

Signs in English and Afrikaans showing designated areas for different races

the African the signs are nothing more than oppressive. They are always there, wherever he turns, to remind him that he is inferior. They shout at him that he is unfit to mingle, unworthy to enter through a certain door, to do business at a certain counter."

Even more frustrating than the color line, the Group Areas Act designated where the different races were allowed to live and work. Asian and colored people who had owned their homes and farms for generations were forced to sell and uproot because Parliament claimed their land was destined as a dwelling spot for some other race. Blacks who lived within walking distance of their jobs in the city had to move to distant townships and spend up to four hours a day commuting on trains that were packed almost to the ceiling with other workers. Many black commuters found themselves arriving home near midnight, yet they had to board buses at 5:00 A.M. in order to be at work on time. They learned to sleep while standing up on crowded buses and trains.

A shop in Johannesburg specializing in identity photos

To control the passage of nonwhites, police cracked down with an expanded "pass law" system. All blacks were required to carry "passbooks" that identified where they lived and where they worked. Failure to produce a passbook (sometimes called a "reference book") at a policeman's demand meant instant arrest. Ernest Cole called the pass law system "the keynote on which enforcement of apartheid is based."

In April 1986, the passbooks were eliminated and replaced by a common identity document issued to all South Africans.

In 1958 the National party Prime Minister Hendrik Verwoerd introduced the plan for putting all the nation's blacks in Bantustans (homelands). "For the first time in their history," declared a government pamphlet "the Bantu [blacks] will realize that the European is prepared to grant them full freedom of progress within their own sphere of life." But even on the surface it was clear the homelands were merely reserve areas for unwanted people. The plan, when fully implemented, would force 72 percent of the country's population into 13 percent of the land area. Also, the homelands gave the government a convenient argument: "Of course blacks can vote. They are all citizens of their homelands and they can vote in their homeland elections."

In theory each of the nation's blacks was assigned a homeland. The millions of urban blacks found they were citizens of a land most had never seen before. But the South African economy was almost entirely dependent upon black labor, and the homelands program had to be enforced in slow stages.

POSTWAR PROSPERITY

Aside from the turmoil brought about by apartheid laws, the rich country of South Africa grew even richer in the 1960s and 1970s. Gold, diamonds, iron ore, coal, and asbestos spewed out of the nation's mines. The cities exploded with a forest of high-rise office and hotel towers.

The factory system expanded with the help of money from American and European corporations. Plants bearing such familiar names as Ford and Volkswagen sprouted up. Due to a government policy that kept both taxes and nonwhite wages low, foreign investors discovered they could earn an astonishing 30 percent return on their investment by manufacturing their products in South Africa.

Postwar prosperity allowed the white middle class and even the white lower class to live a life of luxury unequaled anywhere in the world. The black writer Ernest Cole said of that era, "Hardly a white family in all the land is so poor that it cannot afford at least one or two African servants. Even a Boer of the poorest white

Above: The oil refineries in Durban are located in the industrial area near the port. Below: A diamond mine

Left: A black servant carries the shopping bag for his employer.
Right: Xhosas in a squatters' camp near Cape Town

class, a railroad worker, for instance, will have a servant. On the job he may be only a laborer, but at home he's somebody's boss.''

However, only a tiny proportion of this wealth trickled down to the blacks. During the postwar boom the average black earned one tenth as much as the whites. Nevertheless, blacks streamed to the cities looking for industrial work. For most, city life meant living in one of the many shantytowns that ringed the urban centers.

South Africa's treatment of blacks drew increasing criticism from overseas. Complaints from abroad caused the country to quit the British Commonwealth of Nations in 1961. While the Europeans and Americans denounced apartheid, they saw no conflict in allowing their corporations to earn fortunes under that system. Throughout the 1970s foreign money poured in. By the 1980s one quarter of the stock in South African gold-mining companies was owned by American investors, but there was pressure on stockholders to divest their interests.

THE HOMELANDS

The village of Mathopestad is a dot on the map about 55 miles (89 kilometers) west of Johannesburg. Living there are about two thousand black Africans who are members of the Bakubung culture group. They have farmed the area for more than a century and have had official title to their land since 1911. The soil surrounding the village is adequate and there is ample water for irrigation. The hardworking Bakubung grow corn, sorghum, and beans. They look upon their land as a gift from God.

To government officials Mathopestad is an annoying "black spot" in the middle of a land area designated to be occupied by whites. In 1983 the government ordered the Bakubung to move to what it calls their "tribal homeland." Even though it is called a homeland, few of the Bakubung had ever seen the new land, and no one cares to move there. "It is too hot in the new area and the land is not good," says John Mathope, a leader of the village. "More important, we own the land [we live on] and the ground beneath it. Why should we move when we are happy here?"

The people of Mathopestad refused to move, and in 1986 were battling the order in the courts. What if they lose their case in the white-dominated court system and still resist relocation? "We fear the police will come in the night with guns and force us to go," says Mathope. It has happened before. The police or the army have descended on sleeping villages, rousted the people onto trucks, and dumped them on alien soil. This is one of the tragedies of the homeland program.

Ten rural areas have been designated as homelands. By 1986 four of these homelands had been declared independent by South Africa. When passenger buses cross the borders into independent

	Bophuthatswana
	KwaNdebele
	Lebowa
	Venda
	Gazankulu
	KaNgwane
	Transkei
	Ciskei
	KwaZulu
	Qwaqwa

areas, suitcases are searched and passports are stamped just as officially as if the visitors had left Germany and entered France. But no country other than South Africa recognizes the four homelands as truly independent states. Other nations charge these areas are politically and economically dependent on South Africa, and therefore remain under Pretoria's thumb.

The homelands are generally in the dustiest, most depressed areas South Africa has to offer. The Reverend Desmond Tutu says, "I visited quite a few of those so-called resettlement camps, which is a nice name for dumping grounds for human beings. . . .The able-bodied men are away working as migrant laborers, and the women and the old and the very young try to eke out a miserable existence."

Since the homeland program began, more than three million people have been relocated, many of them by force. The people of the village of Mathopestad tried to go about their work in the mid-1980s, but the fear of being uprooted from a land they love haunted them each day.

CHANGING APARTHEID RULES

A visitor to South Africa in 1984 chatted with the Asian owner of a shop in Johannesburg with two doors fronting the street. Over them were signs announcing WHITE ENTRANCE and COLORED ENTRANCE. Yet whites and blacks walked freely in and out of both doors. When asked about this the owner said, "Oh, I should have taken those signs off years ago. I keep telling myself I'll do it some day when I have the time."

This is an example of changing apartheid. The degree and the particulars of the change vary with the years and with the location. For example, the city of Cape Town integrated its eleven public bathing beaches in 1980, but on the Indian Ocean coast the resort city of Durban still had segregated beaches five years later. Small towns resist changes in racial segregation rules that have been accepted by city people.

The sting of apartheid is still felt by all blacks, but those with money manage to avoid some of the humiliation they had to suffer just a decade earlier. As an example consider the experiences of two blacks visiting Johannesburg in the mid-1980s. One is a businessman who owns several retail stores. The other is an unemployed maid looking for work.

The businessman arrives on an airplane (all flights are integrated) and, providing he can afford it, stays at a large downtown hotel. The higher-class hotels have what are called "international licenses" and can serve all races. The businessman may also eat in the hotel's dining room, but if he wishes to drink a bottle of beer he can do this only in the dining room and only while eating. The law forbids him to enter the hotel bar and mingle with white patrons. If he decides to go to a movie at night, he will have to use a special door and will be seated in the "colored section" of seats. Also, if the businessman wants to use a washroom away from his hotel, he will have to use segregated facilities marked for "nonwhites."

Yet the businessman's plight seems mild compared to the ordeal faced by the unemployed maid. She must ride to Johannesburg on a shabby, dreadfully crowded segregated train. On the train lurk muggers, pickpockets, and purse snatchers. In the city the maid must ride a segregated bus that runs infrequently, and when it comes is packed with passengers. While she waits at the bus stop the maid sees dozens of buses, reserved for whites, that seem to be half-empty. At lunchtime the maid will be served in fast-food hamburger and fish-and-chips stands, but she will be refused in many restaurants. If she does not have the proper identification, she cannot stay in the city at night. So she faces another long train ride where she must cling to her purse and pray no one will steal her precious few pennies.

Still, South African whites contend the old order is changing. They point out that a few years ago the black maid would be arrested if she simply sat down on a bench in a public park. Today she is allowed this tiny privilege. To the whites this is a symbol of progress. To the blacks it is a meaningless concession. "I don't want apartheid reformed," says Nobel Prize-winner Desmond Tutu. "I want the system dismantled."

BLACK RESISTANCE

Speaking at a 1985 mass funeral for eighteen blacks killed during a demonstration, an underground leader named Steve Tshwete declared, "We are going to burn this whole country. We

A photo taken in the 1960s shows the police checking passbooks of blacks.

will destroy everything here, and on the ashes of apartheid a new society will emerge." The audience, with clenched fists held high, chanted back. "Now! Now! Now!"

Starting in 1984, black uprisings that rocked practically every part of the nation blazed across world headlines. Still, it is a mistake to think that black opposition to apartheid is only a recent development. South African blacks were fighting for their rights long before the apartheid laws were drawn up in 1948.

The first political organization to confront the white establishment was the African National Congress (ANC), founded in 1912. The ANC petitioned the government to grant equality to nonwhites, but the organization had little success. In 1959 concerned blacks formed the Pan-African Congress (PAC). The target of PAC's protest was the passbooks South African blacks were required to carry. In March 1960, PAC urged its followers to discard their passbooks and then appear at police stations to invite arrest. In the city of Sharpeville (near Johannesburg) this act of peaceful protest triggered a disaster.

Left: Oliver Tambo unveils a bronze bust of Nelson Mandela, the symbol of blacks' fight against apartheid. Right: Winnie Mandela

A crowd of fifteen thousand people gathered on the lawn of the Sharpeville police station. Many held their hated passbooks in the air, burned them, and dared the police to arrest them. Suddenly one police officer panicked and opened fire without orders. Other policemen followed his lead. The crowd stampeded. When the firing finally stopped, sixty-seven protesters lay dead, and more than one hundred were wounded. Most of the people were shot in the back while desperately running from the scene. Grisly pictures of the massacre appeared in the world press the next day. After the tragedy the South African government praised the police and outlawed both the ANC and PAC.

The Sharpeville killings hardened the attitude of black leaders who had been committed to peaceful protest. One of those leaders was Nelson Mandela, who, after Sharpeville, formed an underground group called the *Umkhonto we Sizwe* (Spear of the Nation). Mandela's group was devoted to sabotage against property, but carefully avoided injuring people. In 1964 Mandela was sentenced to life imprisonment. While languishing in jail he became what many observers believed to be the most influential black figure in South Africa. His wife, Winnie Mandela, has

Left to right: Steve Biko, Albert Luthuli, and Bishop Tutu

carried on this protest. On Christmas Day, 1985, she declared, "If you are black and oppressed in this country, Christmas is a day of mourning."

One mourned black leader is Steve Biko. A decade after Nelson Mandela's imprisonment Steve Biko died in prison after being interrogated by jailers who wanted a confession. Although his body bore scars and he was kept naked and in chains, the jailers denied that Biko was tortured.

One of the few triumphs the black movement achieved came from abroad. In 1960 the Nobel committee in Sweden named Albert Luthuli, president of the ANC, the winner of the Nobel Peace Prize for his efforts to end racial segregation. Luthuli was the first South African black to win the Nobel Peace Prize. Twenty-four years later Bishop Desmond Tutu became the second.

Violence flared up in June 1976 in the notorious black suburb of Soweto. Students there objected to having to learn Afrikaans, calling it "the language of oppression." Protesters were fired at by police, which led to a series of disorders that lasted many months, left hundreds dead, and put thousands of people in jail.

Violence in Sharpeville in 1984

Then, in the middle of 1984, blood spilled again at Sharpeville. Residents there opposed increases in rent payments on their houses. The protests turned ugly and police fired on mobs. The disorders were goaded by the adoption of the new constitution, which continued the policy of denying the black majority political rights. The Sharpeville disturbance touched off disorders that were never quelled. Twelve months later seven hundred people (mostly black) were dead. The majority were killed by police, but post-Sharpeville bloodletting included blacks attacking other blacks they suspected of cooperating with the white establishment.

A hardened new generation that believes it has little to lose leads the street battles against the forces of the government. Angry blacks, some still in grade school, throw rocks at armed police. One young man who calls himself a "freedom fighter" told *Newsweek* magazine, "You haven't seen anything yet. We are just showing the system what we are capable of. It will soon grow beyond stone-throwing."

Encouraging the street battles is the outlawed ANC. The organization, which once advocated peaceful protest, now

Helen Suzlan is an antiapartheid activist.

operates in exile in neighboring countries. In a 1985 interview its president, Oliver Tambo, said, "I fear that [racial war] is not only coming but already here. We will fight and we will expect a blood bath. We will make sacrifices, but then again the West knew it had to make sacrifices when it fought to break the Nazi regime. This regime will be broken, as was Hitler's."

Finally, hundreds of white South Africans oppose their government and fear that the continuation of aparthied will lead to disaster for their country. White opposition includes both English-speaking and Afrikaner people. One opponent is Sheena Duncan, a feisty, gray-haired woman who riles the government with her antiapartheid speeches. She heads a woman's group called the Black Sash, which is dedicated to the liberation of South African blacks. The South African Council of Churches is a multiracial group of churchgoing people who rally against apartheid. Many white leaders of the Anglican church are also bitter foes of government policies.

An avocado plantation in the Transvaal

Chapter 7

WAYS OF LIFE

There is a nonpolitical side to this beautiful land. Despite the turmoil surrounding their institutions, the people work, go to school, read, play sports, and try to enjoy the fruits of a rich country. But the systematic suppression of blacks is such an overwhelming force on people's lives that it bleeds into practically every aspect of the South African story.

LIFE IN THE COUNTRY

Rural South Africa is the domain of either the comfortable or the very poor. And, like so many other aspects of the nation, race separates the haves from the have-nots. The nation's most productive land is owned by a handful of white farmers. The huge majority of black farmers work marginal land, which in the good years can feed their families but provide for little else.

The typical white farmer, whether he is wealthy or merely middle class, is an Afrikaner who can trace the ownership of his land back to the last century. Over the generations the rural Afrikaner's soul has become married to the soil. The passionate bond between farm families and their land gives the Afrikaners the claim that they are as inseparable from the heartthrob of Africa as is any black clan.

Homes of black farm workers in the Orange Free State

Life on the wealthy farms is opulent. The farm family lives in a sprawling house surrounded by a closely shaved lawn that explodes with flower beds. Two or three servants tend to the house, the garden, and the family's personal needs. The larger farms employ a dozen or more field hands (sometimes the black field workers are jail inmates). Despite such huge crews the farm owner uses tractors and other modern harvesting equipment.

Hundreds of middle-class white farmers also work the veld. Their houses are functional rather than elaborate, but they too employ three or four field workers and at least one servant to help in the house.

Black rural life is strikingly different from that of the whites. Their land is suited more for cattle raising than for growing crops on a large scale. The homelands especially consist of dusty, rocky, marginal soil. Malnutrition and infant mortality in the homelands is as appalling as in some of the poorest sections of Africa.

Zulu land, in the state of Natal, is a hauntingly beautiful place where endless green hills roll into the horizon. However, the soil

Two Zulu kraals. *The living quarters, painted white, surround the cattle pens.*

there is strewn with rocks, and waiting for rainfall is a heartbreaking experience for a farmer.

Zulu villages are made up of round mud-brick houses with thatch roofs. Usually the villages are built on a hillside and the houses stand in clusters of four. The clusters are called *kraals.* Zulu traditions allow a man to have more than one wife. The structure of the *kraal* separates each wife's household. On the hillside *kraal* the well-to-do man, who can afford more than one wife, generally lives in the top house while his wives and their children occupy the lower ones. The center of the *kraal* is reserved as a cattle pen.

Family members of the *kraal* household farm a vegetable garden and a cornfield. Corn is an especially important crop for Zulus and practically all rural blacks. Their staple food is a porridge called mealies that is made from corn kernels. For cash the Zulu family trades cattle.

Labor is the primary export of black rural areas. Upon reaching working age almost all black men and women trek to the cities hoping to find a better way of life.

Business section of Johannesburg

THE CITIES

South Africa is an urban nation, with more than one half its population living in cities, suburbs, or townships. Its cities are among the most modern on earth. Almost all the gleaming glass-and-steel buildings were put up during the post-World War II construction boom. The cities have an American rather than a European look about them. Streets crisscross in orderly grid patterns. Shopping malls are common. Suburbs are well developed.

Generally the nation's cities are kept spotless, but they have almost no nightlife. At 5:00 P.M. office workers rush to their suburban homes. The downtown movie houses close their doors at 9:00 P.M. or earlier. In all of Johannesburg there is only one restaurant that stays open all night. City officials, who are usually conservative Afrikaners, disapprove of people carousing into the

Johannesburg is over 5,700 feet (1,750 meters) above sea level.

evening hours. Also, South African urban dwellers live in
constant dread of street crime.

It is not generally known outside the country that fear rules
South African streets. Visitors are warned, ''Don't carry too much
money. Guard your camera. Don't go out at night.'' The warnings
should be heeded because muggers lurk on many shadowy street
corners. Usually the street criminals and their victims are black,
but an unguarded white is always a tempting target, for whites
usually carry more money than blacks do. Despite South Africa's
image as a police-state dictatorship, the streets of Johannesburg
and Cape Town can be dangerous.

The nation's largest urban center is Johannesburg. Most cities
develop along a seacoast or on a riverbank, but Johannesburg
grew above a treasure chest of gold. The original site of Jo'burg (as
the residents call it) was a dusty cow pasture in 1886. Then gold
was discovered, and three years later the empty field was

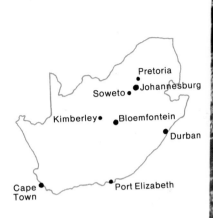

Above: A view of Johannesburg with gold mine slag heaps
Below: White residences in Johannesburg and surrounding areas

Table Mountain in Cape Town is visible to ships from 100 miles (161 kilometers) off shore.

suddenly South Africa's biggest town. Today mine shafts form honeycombs below the city's busy streets. On the outskirts stand pyramid-shaped heaps made up of waste material dug out of the ground in the frantic search for gold. Mineral wealth has given Johannesburg the tallest buildings and wealthiest neighborhoods of any city on the African continent. A flight over the rich suburbs reveals swimming pools glistening like teardrops in practically every backyard. To the wealthy white residents of Jo'burg a pool is as essential as a garage is to the American suburbanite or a formal flower garden to the British country household.

Cape Town, the nation's oldest settlement, is one of the prettiest cities in the world. Its skyline is dominated by the majestic Table Mountain. Nowhere else on earth does the sea encounter the earth so dramatically as at this mountain that fronts South Africa's "mother city." Visitors ride a cable car up the mountainside and roam about its flat top. On the ground one can stroll down

Cape Town lies on the Atlantic Ocean.
Above right: A yacht basin   Below: A flea market

Beautiful beaches of Durban on the Indian Ocean

Government Avenue, which runs across a garden first laid out by Jan van Riebeeck in the 1600s. Along an oak-lined walkway are art museums and graceful century-old government buildings. The colored race was born in Cape Town, and mixed-race people outnumber the city's whites two to one. But the colored in the historic District Six community were forced to move in the 1980s because their neighborhood was declared reserved for white expansion. Still, watching the clouds blow in from the sea and roll over the lofty peak of Table Mountain is an experience burned in the memory of any visitor.

The city of Durban is sometimes called the "Miami of South Africa." It is warm the year round and many residents of harsher climates escape to there during South Africa's winter. The city is built along a strip of silvery beaches. All the beaches are open to the public, but they are split into sections reserved for whites, Asians, colored, or blacks. The most numerous people in the city are Indians. About half a million strong, there are more Indians living in Durban than in any city outside of India. Indians run many of the downtown shops and own restaurants where the tangy smell of curry drifts out of open doors.

Left: A panorama of Durban   Right: Parliament House in Pretoria

Port Elizabeth is South Africa's "Detroit." Here automobiles roll out of giant assembly plants. Industry tends to breed industry, so satellite factories have sprouted up to serve the sprawling automobile centers. Like manufacturing cities anywhere, Port Elizabeth is not a visitors' delight, but the town boasts attractive beaches and an interesting central shopping area.

Although South Africa claims to have three capitals, Pretoria is the center of political power. It is also an unusually attractive town with tree-lined streets and quiet parks. The historic heart of the city is found at Church Square, where its Afrikaner founders built their first church in the 1850s. In the center of the square rises a statue of the revered Afrikaner leader Paul Kruger. Pretoria is the only one of South Africa's great cities where whites outnumber nonwhites. Other cities mirror the country as a whole, and whites are the minority.

Left: A statue of Paul Kruger stands in Church Square in Pretoria.
Right: Young people of Soweto at a public pool

SOWETO

The all-black city of Soweto lies about twenty miles (thirty-two kilometers) from Johannesburg, but the white visitor cannot hop into a taxicab and tell the driver to take him there. Outsiders are forbidden entrance to the city without a special pass.

Instead, an interested traveler must take a special government-run tour bus to see this city that numbers perhaps two million people. "Soweto sounds like an African word," the tour bus guide says, "but really it is a contraction of the words South Western Townships." At the outskirts the visitor sees rows of boxy houses all lined up like soldiers standing at attention. "We're aware these houses appear to be monotonous," says the tour guide, "but you must realize that these people lived in shantytowns just a few years ago. The shacks they once lived in had no plumbing or electricity. These houses are a vast improvement."

Boxlike houses of Soweto

The tour bus stops at a model kindergarten where the visitor watches children being introduced to books. Other stops include a folklore park and a modern shopping center owned and run by blacks. Finally the bus swings past "Millionaires Row"—homes belonging to the handful of Soweto blacks who have grown rich despite apartheid. The tour guide's last comments are, "I wish more foreigners would come here and see for themselves just how well we treat our black people."

However, the tour bus deliberately avoids the vast expanses of Soweto where plumbing is nonexistent, garbage chokes the streets, and crime is outrageous. A deeper understanding of the city can be gained through a book called *Soweto Speaks* written by British-born journalist Jill Johnson, who lived for years in South Africa. Johnson interviewed many residents of this troubled city. "It [Soweto] is a very unhealthy place, a filthy place," says one man.

Left: *The home of a wealthy resident of Soweto*
Right: *A shop in Soweto*

"Sometimes I ask myself why the hell I keep on staying in a place like that . . . and I remember. If you're black you gotta live there."

Soweto is the product of apartheid. The city did not exist before 1948. Then government leaders pointed to a barren spot on the map and determined that most of Johannesburg's black shantytown dwellers should live there. So the match-box houses went up, the shantytowns were bulldozed, and Soweto was born. Over the years Soweto has expanded to include more than 100,000 houses spread out over 200 square miles (518 square kilometers). With few exceptions the residents do not own these homes. They have to pay rent to the government.

Soweto suffers what is probably the worst crime rate of any large city in the world. This typical column appeared in the newspaper the *Daily Sowetan* in 1984: "KILLINGS BRING DEATH TOLL TO 26. Two more people were killed in Soweto Tuesday night, bringing the death toll to 26 since the weekend. . . .In one incident a Zone 4 Meadowlands man collapsed and died at the hospital after being admitted with stab wounds. . . ."

Jill Johnson waited one Friday night at the emergency-room door of that hospital and reported, "By morning up to two hundred mutilated bodies came in. A team of doctors and nurses who have seen it all before, will see it again, worked all night stitching, X-raying, resuscitating, and sometimes certifying the dead." All these were victims of Soweto's never-ending crime war.

The most vicious of Soweto's criminals are roving gangs who call themselves *tsotsis*. Soweto *tsotsis* are coldly casual about committing murder. "If I kill a man it's just unfortunate," one said to Johnson. The *tsotsi* rejects honest work out of hand. Says one, "I can't see the sense of working six days a week for the white man and have him give me a pay envelope [when] I can steal as much in six seconds."

Since they cannot relocate without complicated government approval, the people of Soweto are prisoners in this pocket of poverty and crime. Jill Johnson recorded this line of a poem lamented by a mother whose teenage son had just been knifed to death by *tsotsis*: "Oh, lucky, is the mole that lives in darkness out of touch with the woes of man."

SPORTS AND GAMES

In all societies sports distract a person from his or her troubles. In South Africa they are played with a passion.

The country's national sport is rugby football. Although rugby is an English export, Afrikaners excel at the game. Cricket is a popular team sport among the English-speaking whites. Blacks favor soccer. The Asians are fanatic players of field hockey. Each group has its favorite sport, but white South Africans boast that team sports are among the most integrated activities in the country.

Even though some form of democracy has come to the sports arena, international reaction against apartheid has a powerful impact on the nation's athletes.

In 1984 Zola Budd was a white teenage distance runner who had the habit of running in bare feet. She also had world-class speed and endurance in her events. Budd claimed to have no interest in politics, but being a South African she could not run in the Olympics because the country's athletes have been banned from the games. So Zola Budd went to England and gained British citizenship in order to fulfill her dream to race in the Olympic games of 1984. In Great Britain she was booed, cursed at, and even attacked because she was a hated South African white. Fan reaction grew so violent that some of her races had to be run in secret. Her shabby treatment was another sad case of white South Africans (even those who have no attachments to the apartheid system) being unable to escape the policies of their government.

EDUCATION

Primary-school education is a strictly segregated institution. Blacks go to an all-black school system, colored attend schools especially for mixed-race people, and so on. School segregation extends to the whites, also. Most English-speaking and Afrikaner primary-school students go to separate schools.

Laws require all white children to attend school from ages seven to sixteen. Colored and Asian children must go to school

Left: Cape Town University   Right: Kindergarten students in Soweto

from ages seven to fourteen. Until 1981 no law mandated blacks to attend school, although most of them did so. Now blacks from age six to fifteen must go to school. Because of its far-reaching education laws, most South Africans of all races can read and write. South Africa claims its literacy rate is among the highest of all African nations.

But South Africa's segregated school system fails to provide an equal education for all people. The government's own figures reveal that ten times more money is spent educating a white child than educating a black. A 1982 report states that the average classroom size in white schools was eighteen pupils per teacher, while in black schools that ratio was thirty-nine pupils per teacher.

South Africa boasts several famous colleges and universities. Many of the universities are at least partially integrated institutions. The splendid University of Witwatersrand in Johannesburg has integrated classes. The University of Cape Town lists more than one thousand mixed-race students out of a student body of eleven thousand. Only the Afrikaner-dominated university at Pretoria has resisted integration into the 1980s.

Dr. Christiaan Barnard in 1977 after the publication of his autobiography, Christiaan Barnard: One Life.

PIONEERING IN MEDICINE

In 1967 Christiaan Barnard directed a team of thirty persons in transplanting the first human heart. Dr. Barnard was born in Beaufort West, South Africa. He received his medical training at the University of Cape Town Medical School. Because of his interest in heart surgery, Barnard was invited to do advanced surgical training at the University of Minnesota from 1956 to 1958.

Dr. Barnard's patient, the first person to receive a heart transplant, was Louis Washkansky. The operation was done in Groote Schuur Hospital in Cape Town. Washkansky died eighteen days later because of a lung infection.

Dr. Barnard has pioneered surgical techniques for treating some congenital heart conditions and performed the first double (piggyback) heart transplant.

The Federation of Black Art in Johannesburg

A PASSION FOR THE ARTS

For centuries African people have excelled as sculptors. Black South Africans carry on this tradition. Many sculptors create intriguing figures by combining religious themes with traditional African masks. Others carve marvelous wood creations and make pottery. Blacks also paint dazzling murals on both the outside and inside walls of homes and buildings. Skilled black women weave tapestries that often command high prices at art galleries.

The nation's most celebrated contribution to the arts is its literature. Afrikaner literature began at the turn of the century when Boers such as Jan Celliers and C.L. Liepoldt expressed their sorrows over their people's tragic defeat at the hands of the British. Nadine Gordimer, Alan Paton, and Athol Fugard made up a later group of white writers whose works cried out against their government's treatment of blacks.

The most famous of these protest writers is Alan Paton, whose moving novel *Cry, the Beloved Country* (published in 1948) was the first book to bring the plight of South African blacks to foreign readers. In this passage Paton tells the agony felt by a black mother living in a shantytown and nursing a sick child through the night: "The child coughs badly, her brow is hotter than fire. . . .Quietly my child, oh God make her quiet. God have mercy on us. Christ have mercy on us. White man have mercy on us."

Working early in this century the black South African writer Thomas Mofolo wrote a mystical novel called *Chaka*, based on the life of the warrior king Shaka of the Zulus. In Mofolo's story, supernatural forces tell Shaka he can be lord of all Africa, but his road to glory will be paved with blood. After his many conquests, Shaka is tormented by nightmares. When he dies even the hyenas refuse to touch his body.

Later black and colored writers turned to works of protest. Many found expression in poetry. Perhaps the colored poet S.V. Petersen watched a white person's funeral before writing these lines:

> Blond hair and fair skin,
> Can they take crown and scepter too in death?
> (The pallbearers pace to a death march)
> And darkness waits for you, for me, for both of us.

Above: A painted house in KwaNdebele
Below: Athol Fugard (left) is the author of A Lesson from Aloes *and*
other plays. In New York (right), the actor Zakes Mokae stands in front of
the theater where Fugard's play ran.

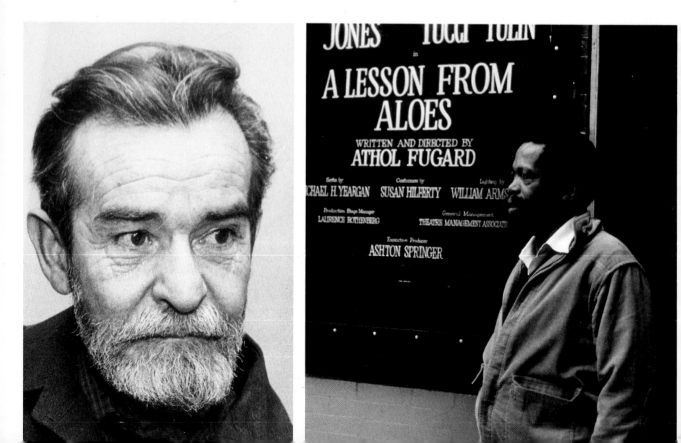

In theater and film, South African writers and directors have won international praise. The play *Master Harold and the Boys*, written by Athol Fugard, was a long-running hit in New York in the 1980s. It presents a tension-filled story about a seventeen-year-old white restaurant manager who has charge over two black waiters twice his age. The three characters are alternately friends, rivals, and finally bitter enemies. Another Fugard play, *Boesman and Lena*, tells of a black couple whose home has been bulldozed to make room for a new township. While walking the countryside looking for new quarters, the homeless couple reflect on their lives together. Zakes Mokae, a black South African actor, won acclaim for his role in Fugard's play *Blood Knot.*

The South African movie *The Gods Must Be Crazy* was a success with world audiences. It tells of a primitive band of San living in a remote South African desert entirely cut off from civilization. Suddenly one of the San discovers a Coke bottle that had been dropped from a low-flying airplane. The bottle is coveted by other members of the clan. The people experience, for the first time in their lives, the powerful emotion of greed. The social order of the entire group is turned upside down.

South Africa has had an odd history with television. For decades the government banned home television, fearing it would be a harmful "outside influence" on their people. The ban was lifted in 1976, and since then home TV exercises almost as powerful an influence in South Africa as it does in the United States and elsewhere. American shows are popular with South African audiences. In 1984 one of the most watched shows on South African TV was the American-produced series called "The A-Team," starring the menacing looking black actor Mr. T.

Chapter 8

SOUTH AFRICA'S FUTURE

In August 1985, President P. W. Botha delivered what was billed as a major policy speech that would outline South Africa's future for years to come. At the time street battles between police and blacks were an almost daily occurrence. Hundreds of blacks had been killed, and many more languished in jail. The racial turmoil was the most destructive in the country's history. Leaders around the world hoped the president's speech would include some new message that could possibly bring peace to South Africa.

For most world leaders, the speech was a colossal disappointment. Mr. Botha called for a general easing of apartheid laws, but announced no dramatic plan to give political power to blacks. He said, "I know for a fact that most . . . reasonable South Africans will not accept the principle of one-man, one-vote, in a unitary system. That would lead to the domination of one [race] over the others and it would lead to chaos."

Left: A facility for whites to train in the use of firearms
Right: P.W. Botha, president of South Africa

After the president's speech, John Kane-Berman, director of the South African Institute of Race Relations located in Johannesburg, said, "This government has run out of steam and out of imagination. They are paralyzed by fear of what would happen to their privileged standard of living, their schools, their religion, their culture. That is the most powerful factor in white politics, and they are not prepared to make a leap of faith to overcome it."

The focus of white fear is the black's desire for political power. Black people are the overwhelming majority in the country. While there are many exceptions, most whites insist that a one-man, one-vote democracy would end white civilization in South Africa. "Why, we'd be overwhelmed," said one white. "I'm a liberal, but give the black man the vote and they'd drive us out of here."

Instead of granting blacks the right to vote, the majority of whites hope to soothe black outrage by gradually easing apartheid rules. But in the 1980s blacks refused to accept concessions on segregation rules in lieu of political rights. As an ANC member told an American journalist, "Be assured the black people are not going to take a half a loaf when they can now see the whole loaf before them."

Black leaders today look beyond apartheid to the time when blacks will either run the country or at least have a powerful political voice in the nation's decisions. But how will they achieve power when the white-dominated government refuses to even discuss giving blacks equal voting privileges with whites? Black opinion varies on this crucial matter. Moderates such as Desmond Tutu urge patience and peaceful protest in the hope that white opinion will bend and a multiracial democracy will emerge in South Africa. Militants such as Oliver Tambo of the ANC urge young people to battle in the streets because ANC members believe peaceful change is an impossible goal.

In 1989 President Botha resigned and F.W. DeKlerk became president. One of the first actions of President DeKlerk was to lift the ban that had outlawed membership in the African National Congress. He also freed Nelson Mandela—after Mandela had spent over a quarter century in prison. Mandela's principal fight has been against apartheid.

Another black South African working against apartheid and for the betterment of his people is Chief Mangosuthu Buthelezi, leader of the Inkatha Freedom party. Buthelezi represents the Zulus, the largest black nation in South Africa.

President DeKlerk has announced plans to demolish all apartheid laws. Mandela and Buthelezi will have to work with DeKlerk. They will have a voice in South African's future, which could be a black-majority government.

Saddleback Pass into the country of Swaziland in the northeast

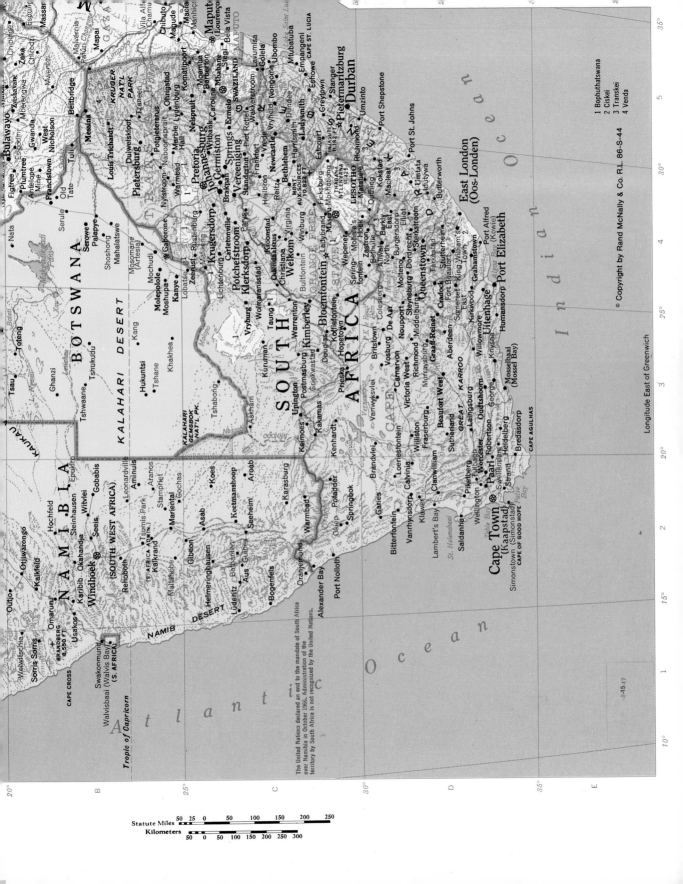

MINI-FACTS AT A GLANCE

GENERAL INFORMATION

Official Name: Republic of South Africa or, in Afrikaans, *Republiek van Suid-Afrika*

Capitals: Cape Town (legislative), Pretoria (administrative), and Bloemfontein (judicial)

Official Languages: Afrikaans and English

Government: South Africa is a republic. The nation is divided into four provinces or states: Cape of Good Hope Province, the Transvaal, Orange Free State, and Natal.

Until 1984 only white citizens 18 years of age and older could vote in parliamentary elections, and only white persons could serve in Parliament. In August 1984 a new Constitution was endorsed creating two separate chambers for colored and Asian representatives but assuming that Parliament would be dominated by white lawmakers.

Under the 1984 Constitution the state president is South Africa's most prominent and powerful government official. He heads the cabinet, which sets the government's policies. He is also the leader of the majority party of Parliament. Members are elected to serve five years unless Parliament is dissolved sooner. The state president, who is elected for a five-year term by Parliament, serves as head of state but has little real power.

The highest court, the Appellate Division of the Supreme Court, hears only appeals. Provincial and local divisions of the Supreme Court hear original cases and appeals from the lower, or magistrates', courts. The white government has set up separate government systems for blacks, colored, and Asians. The government regards the black populations as ten separate nations, each with its own ancestry and culture. They have been assigned reserves known as homelands. Four homelands have been given independence: the Transkei, Bophuthatswana, Venda, and Ciskei. The United Nations does not consider the homelands to be in fact independent nations, and believes that South Africa actually controls them. The Asians have a council called the South African Indian Council.

The National party has controlled the South African government since 1948. It stands for *apartheid*, an Afrikaans word meaning "apartness." Apartheid is official government policy, and represents an effort on the part of a minority government to keep the four racial groups that make up the country apart politically and socially.

Religion: Most Afrikaners belong to the Dutch Reformed Church. As a result, this church is often identified with the government. Most English-speaking whites belong to the Anglican, Congregational, Methodist, or Roman Catholic churches. Most colored people belong to the Anglican, Congregational, Dutch Reformed,

Methodist, or Roman Catholic churches. Most Asians are Hindus or Muslims. About 30 percent of the black people belong to the Anglican, Dutch Reformed, Lutheran, Methodist, and Roman Catholic churches. Many other blacks follow traditional African religions. About 15 percent of the blacks belong to independent Christian churches that combine Christian and traditional African beliefs.

Flag: The South African flag, adopted in 1927, consists of three horizontal stripes; red, white, and blue, with the British Union Flag and flags of the two former Boer (or Dutch) republics set on the white ground.

Coat of Arms: Symbols on the shield represent South Africa's four provinces. The motto, *Ex Unitate Vires*, means Unity Is Strength.

National Anthem: "Die Stem van Suid-Afrika" ("The Call of South Africa")

Money: The basic unit is the rand. In June, 1990 2.64 rands were worth one United States dollar.

Weights and Measures: South Africa is gradually changing over to the metric system.

Population: Estimated 1990 population: 39,550,000; distribution, 55 percent urban, 45 percent rural. Population figure from 1980 census, 28,554,000

Cities:

Cape Town	789,586
Johannesburg	703,980
Durban	677,760
Pretoria	435,100
Port Elizabeth	281,600
Bloemfontein	102,600

(Population figures based on 1980 census)

Homelands: Ten rural areas have been designated as black homelands. Four of them are considered "independent"; Bophuthatswana, Ciskei, Transkei, and Venda. The other six are KwaNdebele, Lebowa, Gazankulu, KaNgwane, KwaZulu, and Qwaqwa.

GEOGRAPHY

Highest Point: Champagne Castle, 11,072 ft. (3,375 m) above sea level

Lowest Point: sea level along the coast

Rivers: The longest river in South Africa is the Orange River, which begins in Lesotho and flows westward about 1,300 mi. (2,090 km) into the Atlantic. The Vaal River, its longest branch, rises in southeastern Transvaal and flows about 750 mi. (1,210 km) before joining the Orange in Cape Province. The Limpopo River begins near Johannesburg and flows about 1,000 mi. (1,600 km) along eastern South Africa and Mozambique before emptying into the Indian Ocean.

Mountains: The Cape Mountain region stretches from the Coastal Strip to the Namib Desert. Mountains run north to south in the west and east to west in the south.

Climate: The seasons in South Africa are opposite to those in the Northern Hemisphere. Most of South Africa has a mild, sunny climate. But there are differences in elevation, wind, and ocean currents that affect the climate in various areas: the Cape Mountains region has warm, dry summers and cool, wet winters. The Coastal Strip tends to have hot, humid summers and dry, sunny winters. In the Eastern Plateau there are hot summer days, but cool nights. In winter, crisp and clear days and cold nights. Most of the rainfall falls in summer; only one fourth of the country receives more than 25 in. (64 cm) of rain a year.

Greatest Distances: East to west—1,010 mi. (1,625 km)
North to south—875 mi. (1,408 km)

Area: 471,445 sq. mi. (1,221,037 km²)

Trees: Indigenous vegetation is divided into five groupings: desert and semi-desert, Mediterranean type, bushfeld (savannah), forests, and temperate grasslands. True desert vegetation occurs only in a narrow strip of 9 mi. (25 km) to 78 mi. (125 km) along the west coast, where rare good spring rains spread spectacular carpets of flowers. Semi-desert vegetation covers most of the western interior. Hardy perennia, shrubs often interspersed with low succulent plants, make good grazing for sheep. Mediterranean-type vegetation consists largely of evergreen shrubs and occurs along the south-western Cape and parts of the south coast. The protea is a wild flower that grows here and is famous throughout the world. Bushveld or savannah (dense thornbush), numerous tree and shrub species, and relatively little grass, occurs in the far north and east. Forest is found in patches along the southern and eastern coastal belts. They include real yellowwood, stinkwood, white pear, black ironwood, assegai, and kamassi.

Fish: More than 60,000 tons of fish are caught and landed every year, more than 90 percent from the cold waters of the Atlantic along the west coast. Anchovy, pilchard, and round herring are processed into fishmeal, fish body oil, and canned fish. Cape hake, kingklip, snoek, horse mackerel, monkfish, club mackerel, sole, and squid are brought in by trawlers; cape rock lobster is harvested along the west coast. Exotic species of oyster are also cultivated.

Animals: South Africa's animal kingdom includes the world's biggest land mammal (elephant), the second biggest (white rhinoceros) and the third (hippopotamus), the tallest (giraffe), and the fastest (cheetah), as well as the world's biggest bird (ostrich) and the largest flying bird (kori bustard). Most animals are protected in game or nature reserves. The best known of the national parks is Kruger National Park in the eastern Transvaal with the largest variety of wild animals, including the elephant, rhinoceros, lion, leopard, giraffe, and the world's largest collection of antelope species.

EVERYDAY LIFE

Food: Whites in South Africa enjoy foods similar to those eaten by Europeans and Americans. They also eat local specialties such as boerwors, an Africaner sausage dish, and curry, an Indian dish of eggs, fish meat, or vegetables cooked with spices. Indians eat curry and other traditional dishes. The basic food of blacks is mealies, which they eat as a porridge.

Housing: Almost 89 percent of all white South Africans live in urban areas and have a high standard of living. They live in homes resembling those of middle-class Americans or Europeans. Some blacks live in round, thatch-roofed houses in the rural areas. Others are in one-room metal sheds in newly designated rural townships. Many build their own temporary shelters while waiting for the opportunity to secure more permanent housing. The housing backlog is most serious among blacks in the urban townships. Many industries provide dormitory-type housing for their employees.

Holidays:

> January 1, New Year's Day
> March 31, Family Day
> April 6, Founders' Day
> May 31, Republic Day
> October 10, Kruger Day
> December 16, Day of the Covenant
> December 25, Christmas
> December 26, Day of Good Will

Culture: English and Afrikaans companies present ballets, concerts, operas, and plays in small towns and big cities. Private black, Asian, colored, and white companies also perform throughout the country.

Commercial theater is well established in Johannesburg, Durban, Port Elizabeth, and Cape Town. South Africa has produced a large number of ballet dancers and choreographers.

Several South African opera singers have a worldwide reputation: Mimi Coertse, Emma Renzi, and Nellie du Toit. There are five professional orchestras. Folk dancing and music are widely performed, and popular music is as prevalent as in any Western country. Before their contact with whites, black music was largely vocal and instrumental; today their serious music is largely choral, and jazz and pop have a large following.

Both blacks and whites writing in English have achieved international recognition and Afrikaans literature is known through the world. South African English authors of note include Alan Paton, Nadine Gordimer, Peter Abrahams, Ezekiel Mphalele, Alex Laguna, Athol Fugard (playwright), and Dennis Brutus, Oswald Ztshali, and Breyten Breytenback (poets). Zakes Mda, a black playwright, won the Amstel Playwright of the Year competition in 1979.

Among the country's greatest art treasures are 3,000 rock art sites where the Stone Age race of Bushmen recorded scenes from their daily lives.

Sports and Recreation: South Africans love sports and their mild climate enables them to spend a good deal of time out of doors. Their favorite games come from England—rugby football, cricket, and association football (soccer). Apartheid has had a severe effect on sports in South Africa. Sports events involving whites and nonwhites have been restricted.

Communication: Radio and television are controlled by the South African Broadcasting Corporation (SABC). Three television channels broadcast in seven languages over 70 transmission stations and 24 booster stations countrywide.

More than 700 newspapers, periodicals, and journals are published regularly. The South African press is the most advanced in Africa. Daily newspapers are published in all of the major cities. The Publications Review Board, a government censorship body, monitors all books, films, plays, and other publications.

Transportation: South Africa has the best transportation system in Africa. About 200,000 mi. (320,000 km) of roads crisscross the country. The government-owned South African Railway operates the country's 14,000 mi. (22,500 km) of railroad track. South African Airways, the government-owned airlines, provides domestic and international service. About 15 major international airlines serve the country. There are well-equipped ports at Cape Town, Durban, East London, and Port Elizabeth.

Schools: Students in each racial group attend separate schools. Most English- and Afrikaans-speaking white children also go to separate schools, although each group must learn both languages. White children 7 to 16 must attend school. More than 90 percent go to public schools. The rest attend government-supervised private schools. About 55 percent of white children complete high school.

Colored and Asian children 7 to 14 must attend school if they live in an area where facilities are available. About 10 percent of the colored children and 25 percent of the Indian children go on to high school. Until 1981, black children were not required to attend school. Under the new system local government councils may request that the national government require black children in their areas between the ages of 6 to 15 to attend school. In the early 1980s, more than 20 percent of South Africa's black children attended school.

South Africa has 11 universities for whites, 3 for blacks, and 1 each for colored and Asians. Students enrolled at universities include about 76,000 whites, 5,200 blacks, 4,400 Asians, and 3,600 colored.

Health: There is one doctor for every 330 whites and one for every 12,000 Africans. Under the new Constitution of 1984, health services will remain segregated and unequal. In the homelands black infant mortality is estimated at between 20 and 25 percent, and malnutrition is severe among children and the elderly. White infant mortality in South Africa is 1.4 percent. South Africa is relatively free of tropical diseases. The world's first human heart transplant was performed by Christiaan Barnard in 1967 at the Groote Schuur Hospital in Cape Town.

Principal Products:
Agriculture: corn, wheat, sugarcane, fruit, peanuts, wool, tobacco
Manufacturing: clothing, processed food, chemicals, plastics, iron, steel, and machinery
Mining: gold, diamonds, asbestos, chromite, copper, platinum, uranium, manganese, iron, coal

IMPORTANT DATES

c. 2000 B.C.—Hunting peoples live throughout much of what is now South Africa

c. A.D. 400—Bantu-speaking farmers begin to enter eastern South Africa

c. A.D. 700—Africans mine copper, iron, and gold

1488—Portuguese discover the Cape of Good Hope

1652—Dutch settlers arrive at site of Cape Town

1814—The Netherlands gives the Cape Colony to Britain

1818—Shaka establishes the Zulu kingdom

1836-38—The Great Trek

1867—Discovery of diamonds

1877—Britain annexes the Transvaal

1879—Britain defeats the Zulu kingdom

1886—Discovery of gold at Witwatersrand

1880-81—The Transvaal Boers defeat the British in the First Anglo-Boer War

1899-1902—Britain defeats the Boers in the Second Anglo-Boer War

1910—The Union of South Africa is formed

1912—African National Congress (ANC) formed to confront white establishment

1920—The League of Nations gives South Africa control of Namibia

1924—In addition to English, Afrikaans becomes official language

1931—Great Britain gives South Africa full independence as a member of the Commonwealth of Nations

1948—The National party comes to power; beginning of apartheid policy

1959—The Pan African Congress (PAC) is formed

1960—Sharpeville massacre; government bans ANC and PAC

1961—South Africa becomes a republic and leaves the Commonwealth of Nations

1966—The United Nations votes to end South Africa's control of Namibia

1971—The International Court of Justice declares South Africa's control of Namibia illegal

1976—Blacks riot in Soweto beginning unrest that still continues

1984—South Africa adopts new constitution; opposition forms under United Democratic Front

1986—Government announces passbooks for blacks are eliminated; tenth anniversary of Soweto protest, government imposes press sanctions and blacks stage large-scale work stoppages

1988—The nation's ultra-right Conservative Party, seeking further restrictions on blacks, gains strength in Transvaal elections

1989—Frederick W. DeKlerk is sworn in as president

1990—President F.W. DeKlerk announces that his government is lifting the thirty-year ban on the African National Congress—the primary black group fighting to end white minority rule—and DeKlerk frees Nelson Mandela, the ANC leader, after twenty-seven years in prison

1991—President DeKlerk announces plans to begin limited integrated schooling, to scrap the remaining laws on which the apartheid system of racial separation was based, and repeal of the 1950 population registration that separated South Africans into four racial categories; DeKlerk proposes a multiparty conference but rejects ANC call for an elected assembly to write the new constitution; however, Blacks still do not have the right to vote

Prime Ministers/State Presidents

Louis Botha	1910-19
Jan Christiaan Smuts	1919-24
James Barry Munnik Hertzog	1924-39
Jan Christiaan Smuts	1939-48
Daniel Francois Malan	1948-54
Johannes Gerhardus Strijdom	1954-58
Hendrik Frensch Verwoerd	1958-66
Balthazar Johannes Vorster	1966-78
Pieter Botha (since 1984, State President)	1978-89
Frederick W. DeKlerk, State President	1989-

IMPORTANT PEOPLE

Christiaan Barnard (1923-   ), surgeon; performed first human heart transplant surgery

Steve Biko (1947-77), founder of the Black Consciousness movement

Allan Boesak, theologian and leader of the United Democratic Front

Pieter W. Botha (1916-   ), president of South Africa

Athol Fugard (1932-   ), playwright

Nadine Gordimer (1923-   ), writer

J.B. (James Barry) Hertzog (1866-1942), founder of the National party; champion of the Afrikaner language

Paul Kruger (1825-1904), statesman; a founder of the Transvaal state and leader of the Boer rebellion

Albert J. Luthuli (1898-1967), reformer; Zulu chief; president of the African National Congress (1952-60); awarded Nobel Peace Prize in 1960

Nelson Mandela (1918-   ), leader of the African National Congress, sentenced to life imprisonment in 1964, but released by DeKlerk in 1990

Thomas Mofolo, author of *Shaka*, a historical romance concerning the founding of the Zulu Empire

Alan Paton (1903-   ), writer and political leader

Cecil J. Rhodes (1853-1902), British administrator and financier; acquired fortune in Kimberley diamond fields

Shaka (c. 1787-1828), founder of Zulu Empire

Jan Smuts (1870-1950), soldier and statesman; prime minister of Union of South Africa from 1919-24, 1939-48

Robert Sobukwe (1924-78), African nationalist, founder of the Pan-African Congress

Bishop Desmond Tutu, Methodist priest; winner of 1985 Nobel Peace Prize

Hendrik Verwoerd (1901-66), architect of apartheid, prime minister from 1958 to 1966

Woman making dolls at Durban market

INDEX

Page numbers that appear in boldface type indicate illustrations

About the Author

R. Conrad Stein was born in Chicago and was graduated from the University of Illinois with a degree in history. He now lives in Chicago with his wife, Deborah Kent, who is also an author of books for young readers, and their daughter, Janna. Mr. Stein is the author of many books, articles, and short stories written for young people.

To prepare for this book Mr. Stein journeyed to South Africa, wandered in the cities and the rural areas, and spoke to people of all races. He found the country to be (in the words of Alan Paton) "something [that is] exciting and depressing, attracting and repelling." It was also one of the most starkly beautiful lands he has visited in a lifetime of travel.